I0181783

Presented to

_____

On _____

By _____

THE ARMOR OF LIGHT

21 Powerful Prayers to Light Up Your Path to Greatness

THE ARMOR OF LIGHT

21 Powerful Prayers to Light Up Your Path to Greatness

Lenie Tibert

Psalm 34:15, *"The eyes of the Lord are upon the righteous, and his ears are open unto their cry."*

If we have a right relationship with God and are earnestly seeking to follow and honor Him with our lives, we never should wonder if He's listening to our prayers. On the contrary, this verse is telling us that God has always listened to the prayers of His faithful servants.

CONTENTS

PREFACE

Dear Friend,

I am thrilled with the book you are holding in your hands at this moment. This book is designed to help feed your inner spirit with the Word and intensify your prayers. Also, it is intended to encourage and heighten your prayer life. It is my sincere prayer that this book helps you become more consistent in the Word, that it may evoke the Power of the Holy Spirit to erupt in you and instantaneously bring the devil to his knees. From firsthand experiences, I have seen the manifestation of the Power that has transformed individuals to transcend from faith to faith, glory to glory, victory to victory, and eventually, to fight for victory for the rest of their lives.

Prayer is a gift from God that when used properly, will yield great victory in our lives. God loves you and gives you His Word so that you can have great results in your prayer life. Pray with confidence in the Word, know that God loves you and He will answer *ALL* your prayers.

ACKNOWLEDGMENTS

I give thanks to my Lord and Savior, the Author and the Finisher of my faith. Thank You, my Lord, for clothing me with Your strength and courage as I birth this purposeful and spiritual assignment.

INTRODUCTION

EVERYONE WHO LONGS FOR powerful and victorious life instinctively understands that the root of their power and authority lies only in prayer. God calls on His people to pray many times throughout the Scripture. This Almighty, powerful God cries out, "*Oh! If only my people will call out to me. If only they will turn to me from their sinful ways. If only they will lift their eyes to me,* only then! *Then, I will hear their cries and heal their land.*" (2 Chronicles 7:14)

His people, Called by His name. Do you realize what power there is in being called by His name? Do you realize that all Heaven and all of Earth and all of Hell *tremble* at the name of the King of kings and Lord of lords? The one Name that is above every other name; the name before which every knee *must* bow, and every tongue *must* confess; Jesus is Lord.

When anyone in the Spiritual realm looks at you, do you know what they see? They see the Blood of Jesus, the

Son of God, and the Light of the world, God Himself, in you. They see that you belong to the King of the Heaven. And they shudder in terror and awe.

The Amazing Gift of Prayer

Praying for a few minutes a day may not seem like much at all, but it matters a great deal in the spiritual realm. You are not warring against flesh and blood—you are warring against the powers and forces of the enemy (Ephesians 6:12). God is with you, and if God is with you, no one can stand against you, (Roman 8:31).

Was it not He who said, "Ask, and you will receive?" (Mat 7:7) Was it not your God who said, not once, not twice, not even three times but *four* times in the *same* speech, that if you abide in Him, you can ask for anything according to His will and He *will* do it? (John 14:13, 14; 15:7, 16) Just a few minutes of your time each day spent in faith-filled prayer will be answered. That's not just anyone's words, that's what the Lord Himself said, and that's what He promised (Mat 21:22). He doesn't lie, and He doesn't go back on His word (Num 23:19).

You are indeed the Lord's Remembrances, and it is a privileged position. Only His children have access to His throne. Only you who have been redeemed by the precious Blood of Christ, you who have been made righteous because that same Blood can come boldly before the Holy, Almighty God, Creator of the Universe and speak to Him. And He actually *listens!* How amazing is that!

How the Destroyer Works: Through Sin

Remember that the thief comes only to steal, kill, and destroy you. Do not be ignorant of his schemes and think that because you gave your life to Jesus, you are now free from the traps of the enemy. Satan is a deceiver, and if you have pockets of sin in your life that you are feeding even after you have been saved, he will latch on to them. And as much time as you ignorantly think that you do not have to worry about him because you have been saved, he will continue to take advantage of you. There is a reason God says that His people are destroyed from lack of knowledge. They are *His* people, called by *His* name. How can they be completely destroyed? The Destroyer is still working in their lives through their ignorance. This is the reason why there are so many Christians who are struggling in their lives. They do not live in the peace and joy Christ offers because of roots of unconfessed sins in their lives that they haven't dealt with and which Satan is taking advantage of.

Jesus won the victory once and for all on the cross. You are aware that the angels know that, Satan and the demons know that. However, if you do not enforce that victory in your life by vigilantly guarding yourself against sin and confessing all sins to Jesus and accepting forgiveness for them, Satan will take advantage of you.

You must understand just how insidious and grave sin is to God and how powerful a tool it is for Satan before you can grasp the magnitude of what is happening in the spiritual realm.

It is easy for Christians to dismiss the power of sin because of the forgiveness of sin and the love of Jesus that is readily available to those who ask.

Sin was so entrenched in you that only God could free you from it. Knowing what He would have to let sin into Himself in those final moments, Jesus spent His last hours tormented in the garden, so agonized that His sweat was His own Blood. Sin was so *abhorrent* to God that the moment it touched the Son, the Father had to tear Himself away from Him. That separation led to the scream of desperation that left Jesus' lips with His final breaths—ABBA! ELOI! FATHER! Don't leave me!

Does sin not do that to you? Do you realize just how horrible sin is? It is not something that is to be taken for granted. Even a small lie is sinful. No matter how you try to justify it, it does not change the fact that sin is a sin. That sin caused Jesus to suffer. That sin caused Jesus to be separated from the Father. That sin caused Jesus to *die a horrific death*. That sin allowed Satan the opportunity to torment Jesus.

If sin has that much power to affect God himself, why do you think you are immune to it? Why do you toy with it and allow Satan an entryway into your life? Satan was so eager to get access to Jesus that he actively *tempted* Him three times! Why do you think you have escaped his clutches?

Praise God that you are saved, but do not be so naive to believe that Satan no longer has access to your life. Look at Peter. Satan approached God and asked to sift him like wheat. Jesus warned Peter of the interaction and said that He had prayed for Peter that he might be strong and would strengthen his brothers *after he had turned back*. Satan was permitted to approach Peter! Jesus had to pray and intercede for Peter. Peter still failed. Peter still denied Jesus because Peter was not on guard against Satan. That same Peter warned other Christians years later, *"Be sober-minded and alert. Your adversary, the devil, prowls around like a roaring lion, seeking someone to devour. Resist him, standing firm in your faith . . ."* (1 Peter 5:8–9).

As a prayer warrior, you need to be alert to the Devil and his schemes always. You can pray night and day, but if there is unconfessed sin in your life, you are ineffective. Each time you pray, confess your own sins first and foremost before you intercede for others.

God's Promises to the Warrior

Now that you have laid the private foundation for your prayers, you need to know and claim God's promises about prayer. In 1 John, we are told, *"This is the confidence we have in approaching God: that if we ask anything according to his will, he hears us, and if we know that he hears us—whatever we ask—we know that we have what we asked of him"* (v 14, 15). That is an amazing promise. If you ask Him *anything*, He will do it for you if it aligns with His will. How do you know what His will is? You know it only by abiding in Him. When you continually *live* in Jesus, His heart and desires become your very own and you begin to want and pray for only the things that honor and please God. That is why the psalmist boldly declares in Psalm 37:4, "Commit your way to the Lord, and he will give you the desires of your heart."

God promises in Jeremiah that when you seek Him, you will find Him, as much time as you seek Him with all your heart. (Jer. 29:13). This falls in line with Matthew 7:7, *"Ask and you will receive, seek, and you will find, knock, and the door will be opened to you."*

Similarly, Jesus promises that *"Whatever you ask for in prayer, believe that you have received it, and it will be yours."* (Mk 11:24) That is an incredible promise. When you pray, pray with faith knowing that God is a good Father and He gives good gifts to His children. Receive what you are praying for before it even comes into being, praise God for it, and it will be yours if it is in keeping with His will for the situation.

When Jesus taught the disciples to pray in Mathew 6, He emphasized these things that were just discussed.

Seeking the will of God: "Your kingdom come, your will be done, on earth as it is in heaven.

Repentance: "Forgive us our debts …"

Humility and Obedience: "As we have also forgiven our debtors."

Being on Guard: "Lead us not into temptation but deliver us from evil."

These aspects of prayer in the life of the warrior are not just general pointers but so vital to the effectiveness of prayer that Jesus made sure to include them in the five short sentences He used in His instructions to His disciples, so they too could model their prayers after His and be effective.

Years later, John and Peter based their instruction to the churches in the matter of prayer on these foundational truths. Even Paul, who repeatedly commands, "Pray without ceasing" contends these truths in his epistles. In Colossians 1, Paul prayed to God that he would "Fill (the church) with the knowledge of (God's) will in all spiritual wisdom and understanding so that (they would) live worthily of the Lord and please him in all respects—bearing fruit in every good deed, growing in the knowledge of God, being strengthened with all power according to his glorious might for the display of all patience and steadfastness." (v. 9–12)"

ONE

THE ARMOR OF GOD (EPH. 6:10–18)

IN EPHESIANS 6, APOSTLE Paul defines the spiritual clothing of armor: the belt of truth, the breastplate of righteousness, sandals of readiness grounded in the gospel of peace, the shield of faith, the helmet of salvation, and the sword of the Spirit. The armor prepares us for battle against the spiritual force of evil. God provides for our defense against attacks, and He gives us the offensive weapons of His Word and prayer. We need to be equipped with the armor of God.

To be a well-prepared prayer warrior, you need to gather up your armor and weapons. Familiarize yourself with the armor of God described in Ephesians 6:10–18.

Out of all the pieces of armor described in Ephesians 6, only one of them is a weapon. Every other piece of equipment is defensive and meant to protect you from attack. The only weapon you need against the enemy is *"the sword of the Spirit, which is the Word of God."*

Have you ever prayed the Scripture before? An

example was in the book of Acts when they recited a part of the Psalmist. When you pray the Scripture, you pray the words of God. When Jesus fought Satan's temptations, He fought by using the Scripture and Satan could not stand against the truth of it. He *did* mimic Jesus' technique in the third temptation when he told Jesus to jump off the temple because God had promised (in Psalms) that He would *"command his angels to lift you up in their hands so that you will not strike your foot against a stone."* That was true; God had promised that, but Jesus also knew that God had said, *"Do not put the Lord your God to the test."*

Satan knows the Scripture inside and out, and he uses and twists its truth for his own purpose—to steal, kill, and destroy you. That is why it is vital that you are in the Word every day, allowing the Holy Spirit to teach you so that you too can withstand the wiles and guiles of the enemy.

You are in a war every day of your life. You cannot see the forces of God and Satan battling, but you understand the consequences and effects all around you. Satan's only purpose is to destroy the people God created. All the world and all its inhabitants save those who have trusted in Jesus for their salvation, are under the power of the enemy. God has entrusted us with authority in Jesus' Name in this battle to war against demons and principalities through prayer. The only way we can survive is to put on our armor every single day whether we are actively involved in prayer or not. A soldier on active duty is never out of his uniform. We are *always* on duty. We should never be out of uniform. EVER! It is the only thing protecting us.

That is why the Scripture instructs us to always pray in the Spirit. You need to change your perspective to see that prayer and warfare are not relegated to a specific time or day of the week. If you could see the barriers, blockades, chains, and weapons the enemy is employing against you, would you sit quietly sipping your coffee and chatting with your friends? If you knew that the only way to avoid those fiery arrows was to praise and worship God and speak the Word of truth, you would be singing at the top of your lungs, hands high in the air and feet dancing over the ground. Rejoicing every time an arrow fell to the ground uselessly, every time a chain was broken, and a barrier destroyed, and an enemy rendered incapacitated. You can't see it, but it is no less real. Act like it!

Cover yourself then! Put on your belt, breastplate, helmet, and shoes. Take up your shield and sword. Are you really going to go into battle unprepared? Your first and the best defense are your faith; it is the shield that deflects all the bullets and swords the enemy rains over your field. Do you really think you will survive on your own righteousness? Put on the righteousness of God to protect your heart. Put on your helmet, the salvation God gave you, to protect your mind. Speak out and proclaim the truth, it is the belt that buckles your breastplate around your hips for a reason! Gird yourself with the Word of Truth. And don't you dare try to walk on those hot coals with bare feet! Put on your shoes! Proclaim the gospel to the prisoners enslaved behind enemy lines. Run and carry them on your shoulders to safety. And fight! Brandish that sword like the warrior you are. Let the Word be your battle cry as you engage the enemy. No mercy! No Surrender! Obey your Commander, follow His guidance, and you will prevail. Climb over and demolish, with every step, every stronghold of the enemy. Set the captives free. Rescue them from the fire. Fight for your God, your King and advance His kingdom forcefully.

The Armor of God, Prayer:

Father in the Name of Jesus, let the words of my mouth, and the meditation of my heart, be acceptable in Your sight. I put on the whole armor of God so that I can stand firm against the attacks of the enemy. I place around my waist the belt of truth. I am free from the schemes and plans of the enemy. I put on the breastplate of righteousness. I declare, I am the righteousness of God, You took my sin at the cross and gave me Your righteousness, *"Therefore, as Your chosen people, holy and dearly loved, I clothe myself with compassion, kindness, humility, gentleness, purity, understanding, patience and kindness, in the name of Jesus."* (Colossians 3:12)

Thank you, oh God for the power of the Holy Spirit,

that I am able to stand and do Your work and speak the Word with great boldness and confidence. Father, according to Your Word, "thy word is a lamp for my feet, a light on my path." I declare and decree, I stand strong with unshakable faith. According to Romans 8:37–39 we are more than conquerors through Him who loved us. For I am persuaded that neither death nor life, nor angels nor principalities nor powers, nor things present nor things to come, nor height nor depth, nor any other created thing, shall be able to separate us from the love of God which is in Christ Jesus our Lord.

I declare, nothing can separate me from the love of Jesus. I am prepared and equipped to face any trouble that the enemy throws at me. Hallelujah! Therefore, in the Name of Jesus, I strap on my feet the gospel of peace in preparation [to face the enemy with firm-footed stability and the readiness produced by the Good News]. I put on the garment of faith to defeat the attacks of the enemy. I put on Jesus Christ. I put on the Armor of Light. Satan, I rebuke and resist you, in the Name of Jesus. I cut off your tongue; I stomp on your head, you are under my feet. I declare, the Lord is my rock and my fortress and my deliverer, my God, my rock, in whom I take refuge; my shield and the horn of my salvation, my strong tower. I call upon the Lord, who is worthy to be praised, and I am saved from my enemies (Ps. 18:2–3).

I put on the helmet of salvation and the sword of the Spirit, which is the word of God. I put on the helmet of hope, the helmet of peace, and the helmet of love on my head; I wrap myself with zeal.

I decree every witchcraft, curse, and spell over my life are reversed. I demolish the works of every witch, warlock, evil power, voodoo, black and white magic, and all other powers of darkness in the Name of Jesus. I take authority over Satan's kingdom. We command every stronghold to be broken and go back to the pits of hell in the Name of Jesus.

I walk untouchable; I walk in the FIRE of the Holy Ghost. We walk with the Authority and the Spirit of Christ. We put on the whole armor of God, nothing and no one can touch us. I am untouchable, in Jesus' Mighty Name.

This prayer is sealed with the Blood of Jesus.

Amen!

Two

PRAYER FOR PROTECTION

WHEN WE GO THROUGH times of trouble, the prayer of Psalm 91 is comforting and efficient when we say it from the heart and are in good standing with God. Protection is a solid promise of God. Protection means that God will give you a way to escape the schemes of the enemy every time he rears his ugly face at you. The devil hates God and how dead serious he is on destroying God's Kingdom. He hates everything in the world that reminds him of God and of what he lost. He hates you; he hates me. The devil has no real power; he can't just come roaring in and ripping things up anytime he wants to. If he could, he would have done that a long time ago. He cannot go in there and start destroying and stealing from you unless he gets you into a place of sin, disobedience, doubt or ignorance. The Bible says he's bound to thoughts that are common to men, in other words, he uses people to get his work done for him. Praise God! We are not bound, we are FREE! We fight our warfare with unique weapons. So, if he's giving you troubles, pull out the weapons God has given you, the weapon of the Word, the weapon of Prayer, the weapon of Faith, and use them to tie him in knots. Then and only then he will not stand a chance.

A Personal Prayer for Protection from Psalm 91:

Father, I praise You as I dwell in the secret place of the Most High and as I shall abide under the shadow of the Almighty. I will say of the Lord, "He is my refuge and my fortress; My God, in You I will trust." Surely, You shall deliver me from the snare of the fowler. And from the perilous pestilence.

You shall cover me with Your feathers, and under Your wings, I shall take refuge; Your truth shall be my shield and buckler. I shall not be afraid of the terror by night, nor of the arrow that flies by day, nor of the pestilence that walks in darkness, nor of the destruction that lays waste at noonday. A thousand may fall at my side, and ten thousand at my right hand; but it shall not come near me. Only with my eyes shall I look and see the reward of the wicked. Because I have made You, who are my refuge, the Most High, my dwelling place. No evil shall befall me, nor shall any plague come near my dwelling; for You shall give Your angels charge over me, to keep me in all my ways. In their hands, they shall bear me up, lest I dash my foot against a stone.

I shall tread upon the lion and the cobra, the young lion and the serpent I shall trample underfoot. Because I have set my love upon You, therefore You will deliver me; You will set me on high because I have known Your Name. I shall call upon You, and You will answer me; You will be with me in trouble; You will deliver me and honor me. With long life, You will satisfy me and show me Your salvation. (Psalm 91 NKJV)

THREE

PRAYERS FOR HEALING

THE BIBLE SPEAKS OF miraculous healing through the work of Jesus Christ and faith in God. Prayer has healing power. James commands us, "Is any sick among you? Let him call for the elders of the church; and let them pray over him, anointing him with oil in the name of the Lord" (James 5:14). God is compassionate and merciful; He is Jehovah-Rapha "(The God Who Heals)." Jesus healed the woman who had "a spirit of infirmity eighteen years, and was bent over and could in no way raise herself up. But when Jesus saw her, He called her to Him and said to her, "Woman, you are loosed from your infirmity." And He laid His hands on her, and immediately she was made straight, and glorified God (Luke 13:10–13)." Jesus healed the woman who had been bleeding for 12 years; He said to her, "Daughter, your faith has made you well. Go in peace, and be healed of your affliction (Mark 5:34). When Jesus healed the blind man who sat by the road begging, Jesus said, receive your sight; your faith has made you well." And the Bible says, immediately he received his sight (Luke 18:35–43). And let's not forget about Jairus who requested healing for his daughter, Jesus said, "*Do not be afraid; only believe, and she will be made well*" (Luke 8:50). On the one hand, healing power can only come from faith in Jesus. The book of Acts eloquently says, "By faith in the name of Jesus, this man whom you see and know was made strong. It is Jesus' name and the faith that comes through him that has completely healed him, as you can all see" (Acts 3:16).

Prayers for Healing:

Father, we come into Your presence in the Name of Jesus Christ. For Your Word says when two or more are gathered, there You are in their midst. Father, You are our healer; You are our deliverer, You are our miracle worker. According to Psalm 103, you are the One who forgives all our iniquities; You are the One who heals all our diseases, You are the One who redeems life from destruction, who crowns with loving kindness and tender mercies, who satisfies our mouth with good things so that our youth is renewed like the eagles.

Your word says in Isaiah 53:5 that you were wounded for our transgressions, bruised for our iniquities; the chastisement of our peace was upon You, and by your stripes we are healed. Peter says You bore our sins in Your own body on the tree, that we, being dead to sins, should live unto righteousness, by whose stripes we were healed.

I stand on Your promise, Father, that healing is the children's bread. I declare that I am Your child, and I am worthy to receive more than just the crumbs that fall from Your table. You are Jehovah-Rapha, the God who heals, and You have the final word on my destiny. I declare that I am healed in the Name of Jesus. I command all sickness, all diseases, and all pain to leave my body right now! I decree I will live my life sickness free, disease free, pain-free, stress-free, and therefore I speak complete healing over my body. Father Your word says in Jeremiah 17:14, *"Heal me O LORD my God and I shall be healed, save me O LORD and I shall be saved, for you are my praise."*

I speak directly to the sickness and disease and call them by name. Spirit of depression, get out of my thoughts! Demon of Cancer, get out of here! All types of tumors, heart disease, heart attack, chest pain, stroke, migraine headache, gonorrhea, hepatitis, HIV/AIDS, herpes, chlamydia, arthritis, asthma, common cold, obesity, sickle-cell anemia, blood disorder, high blood pressure, and diabetes, get out of my body and my loved ones, and I command you to die, NOW! In the Name of Jesus.

I go to the root cause of the problem and command the source of this sickness and disease to die and disappear at once, in the Name of Jesus. I command every ungodly spirit assigned at the root to be cast out NOW, in Jesus Name. I command fire from heaven to be released and consume every ungodly agreement I may have made consciously or unconsciously that would open the door for the enemy to enter and cause affliction. I command those doors to be closed now, in Jesus Name. Father, right now I declare I am blessed and healed. I claim full and complete healing. You are the Great and only Physician who says that by His stripes we are healed. You are our strength, You are our encourager, You are our deliverer, You are our Savior. Therefore, I trust you.

Father as I close this prayer, I ask that all of this be done for Your glory in Jesus' Name! I shall live, and not die, to declare the works of the LORD (Psalm 118:17).

Amen!

FOUR

PULLING DOWN OF STRONGHOLDS

STRONGHOLDS ARE FORMED IN our minds what is known as an image, that is, a false thought that we believe to be true, but in reality, is not.

> *"For though we walk in the flesh, we do not war after the flesh: For the weapons of our warfare are not carnal, but mighty through God to the pulling down of strongholds. Casting down imaginations, and every high thing that exalteth itself against the knowledge of God, and bringing into captivity every thought to the obedience of Christ."*
>
> 2 CORINTHIANS 10:3, 4–5

The strongholds of historical landmarks all had towers in every corner of the building, and they had one tower that stood taller than all the rest. The chief watchman stationed himself on the tallest tower. From his position, he could see every part of the territory he protected. He could see far beyond even the boundaries of his property. When the enemy tried to approach from any side, he could see them from quite a distance, and he knew exactly how many men they had. He had time to signal their approach and could send enough soldiers to guard that site against attack.

You are a watchman as well. Your high tower is Jesus. Station yourself in that throne room so you can watch over your territory. The Spirit will tell you when invaders are coming and how they are advancing against you. You can have your counter-attack in place well before they reach you. You have just reinforced your victory. What happens though, if you are not in the high tower when the enemy is sighted? How can you protect your territory if you are not even on the grounds, to begin with?

Anne Graham Lotz said in her book, *The Daniel Prayer*, "Prayer which moves Heaven is a commitment to pray that is confirmed by God's Word, while the compulsion to pray is often triggered by our problems." If you want to pray in a manner that moves heaven and routes the devil, you need to be committed to prayer, not just praying when you "need" to pray. Your commander and chief will only send you into battle if you are dependable. If you flake on Him or only come running to Him when you see the danger, then why should He trust you with the life and burdens of His precious saints? Because of His mercy, you may narrowly escape the arrows of the enemy, but you will never experience the victorious life of the watchman who defeated his enemy when they were still far away from his territory.

Jesus says that Satan is a murderer, a liar and the father of lies (John 8:44). God reminds us to stay aware of Satan's schemes, to be alert, and stay close to Him. When Satan tells you lies, contradict him with the Word of God. The Bible reminds us, *"Submit yourselves therefore to God, resist the devil, and he will flee from you"* (James 4:7). Start making the devil feel uncomfortable for a change. You have the authority to do so. You have the power to destroy his schemes. You have so much power in you that every time you wake up, the devil should wail, *"Oh no! That troublemaker is at it again!"*

Spiritual Warfare Prayer:

Father in the Name of Jesus, let there be FIRE in my mouth as I advance in this prayer. You are my fortress; my high tower, and my deliverer; my shield and in You I trust (Ps 144:2). All praise and honor belong to You, our High Priest.

I decree and declare that the weapons of my warfare are not carnal, but mighty through God. I pull down strongholds; I cast down imaginations, and every high thing that lift themselves against the knowledge of God, and I bring into captivity every thought to the obedience of Jesus Christ. I put on the full armor of God, the belt of truth buckled around my waist, with the breastplate of righteousness in place, and with my feet fitted with the readiness that comes from the gospel of peace. In addition to all this, I take up the shield of faith, with which I can extinguish all the flaming arrows of the evil one. I take the helmet of salvation and the sword of the Spirit, which is the word of God.

I send every curse and demonic attack back to their senders. I use my weapons against the kingdom of darkness. I shut down every door that the devil may have opened in us from evil contacts. *Jesus became a curse on the cross for us and blotted out the handwriting of ordinances that was against us, which was contrary to us, and took it out of the way, nailing it to his cross*" (Colossians 2:14). I decree and declare that the works of darkness are destroyed. I take authority over dark powers, Jezebel, false prophetic words, manipulators, witches, soul ties, lying spirits, lying dreams, and lying visions in the Mighty Name of Jesus. I speak that the Holy Spirit anointing takes away every burden and destroy every yoke in my life and my loved ones.

I bind and cast down rulers of the darkness of this world and spiritual wickedness in High Places. I destroy any spiritual strongholds in my life. I command them to die NOW in the Name of Jesus. Like Elijah called forth FIRE from heaven, I too call forth the FIRE of the Almighty God to burn the works of Satan. Satan! I rebuke you. I burn you with the Fire of the Holy Ghost. I burn the spirit of divination, black and white Magic, witchcraft, physical disease, mental disease, spiritual battle, in the Name of Jesus.

Right now, Father, I call forth thousands of angels to protect us, to guide us, to encourage us, and to strengthen us, in the Name of Jesus. I call forth the *"chief angel"* Michael, to draw his sword and begin to fight the forces of evil.

I decree and declare I am free from the strongholds of the enemy by the Blood of Jesus Christ. I decree and declare Psalm 138:7, *"Though I walk in the midst of trouble, You will revive me; You will stretch forth Your hand against the wrath of my enemies. And Your right hand will save me."* According to Psalm 23:4, *"Though I walk through the valley of the shadow of death, I fear no evil, for You are with me; Your rod and Your staff they comfort and console me."*

Therefore, Devil! I command you in the Name of Jesus, let go everything that belongs to me. Devil! You have no authority over my physical, my spiritual, and my emotional being. You are a liar and you are defeated in the Name of Jesus.

Amen!

FIVE

PRAYER FOR FINANCIAL BREAKTHROUGH

BREAKTHROUGH IS A WORD we hear quite often in the Christian church. According to the freedictionary.com breakthrough is defined as: "An act of overcoming or penetrating an obstacle or restriction. A military offensive that penetrates an enemy's lines of defense. A major achievement or success that permits further progress, as in technology." Definition of a *breakthrough* for English Language Learners: "A sudden increase in knowledge, understanding, etc., an important discovery that happens after trying for a long time to understand or explain something, a person's first significant success. In other words, you need to decide to move beyond the limitations that the enemy has taken you.

Sometimes it is hard to trust God especially when we do not see any changes in our finances. We exercise our faith only when we are going through trials and tribulations which force us to rely on God. Financial challenges and other issues can be some of the most stressful seasons in our life because God wants to reveal Himself as the provider (Jehovah Jireh), the promise-keeper, the supplier, and the breadwinner.

As children of the highest God, we have the power to declare and decree into the spiritual atmosphere and command prosperity to manifest in our lives. Prophetic declaration is a powerful tool we need to have and understand. We need to have faith when we do this because *faith is the substance of things hoped for, the evidence of things not seen* (Hebrews 11:1). If you can see it, you can have it. Just believe it.

When we desire prosperity in our lives, we need to keep confessing, decreeing, and declaring until it becomes a reality in our lives.

Prayer for Financial Breakthrough:

Father, You are the King of kings and the Lord of lords. You reign over all the earth. Worthy is Your precious Name. I praise and glorify You. Your Word declares that if I delight myself in the Lord, therefore, I am blessed. Wealth and riches shall be in my house, and my righteousness endures forever (Psalm 112:1–3).

Father, I thank you for giving me prosperity in every area of my life. I decree and declare that I am blessed, there is no lack in my house, all my needs are met in the Name of Jesus. I declare that I am debt free. I am not only blessed, but I am a blessing to others. I decree a season of unmerited favor, a season of more than enough, a season of overflow. I burn and destroy the walls of poverty in my life. I claim all that Jesus has for me. I command you, Devil, to lose the wealth of this earth. Take your hands off my finances, off my businesses, and off my successes! I command that wealth and riches locate me right now in the Name of Jesus. Father, you are the Lord of my life, You are the Lord of my finances.

The Scriptures make it clear that, *"The blessing of the Lord makes rich, and he adds no sorrow to it."* Therefore, I declare that my season of frustration, failures, and disappointments are over. I walk into a new season of supernatural blessings, supernatural miracles, prosperity and divine appointments. I declare and decree new season and new prosperity. I call forth supernatural financial blessings into my life, in the Name of Jesus.

Father, I thank You that I am heir to the BLESSING of Abraham. According to Galatians 3:29, *"If I belong to Christ, then I am Abraham's seed, and heirs according to the promise of God."* As a joint heir with Christ Jesus, I claim all that God has for me because He promised that whatsoever I ask the Father in the name of the son, He will give it to me. I stand in unshakable faith. I am ready to receive from my Supplier. I stand on Psalm 34:10, *"The young lions lack and suffer hunger; but those who seek the Lord shall not lack any good thing."* Father, as I seek Your face, I believe that I lack no good thing.

I declare, I am the HEAD and not the tail, I am the LENDER and not the borrower, I am blessed in the city, and I am blessed in the field. When the enemy comes against me, the Spirit of God will raise a standard against him. Therefore, I receive now by faith the hundredfold returned to me by the enemy. Satan! In the Name of Jesus, I rebuke you! I burn you with the Fire of the Holy Ghost. I command you to take your filthy hands off my businesses, finances, relationships, family, ministry, and my health NOW! I declare that the harvest belongs to me, and it is mine! Everything that God has for me is for me, and I receive all in the Name of Jesus.

Father, Your Word says in Ephesians 3:20 that "*You are able to do exceeding abundantly above all that I ask or think, according to the power that worketh in me.*" I have Faith and Power in this season. "*You promise you will supply all my needs according to Your riches in glory by Christ Jesus.*"

I command, anyone and anything that is not of God trying to frustrate me, hinder me, or hurt me in the name of Jesus to go back to the pit of Hell. I tear down the spirit of poverty out of my bloodline. I speak increase, more than enough, overflow into my finances. I decree and declare a fresh anointing into my life, into my finances, into my health, and into my business. I release new ideas, new business plans, I declare my business will come alive, my ministry will come alive, in Jesus' Name.

Amen!

A Personal Prayer for Blessing from Deuteronomy 28:1-14

The Spirit of God is going to move mightily in your finances. You are heir to the blessing of Deuteronomy 28:1–14.

Father, you are Jehovah Jireh, our Provider. You are our Supplier; You are our Way Maker, You are our never-ending Source. According to Deuteronomy 28:1–14, *"If I diligently obey the voice of the Lord my God, observe carefully all His commandments which He commands me today, that the Lord my God will set me high above all nations of the earth. Moreover, all these blessings shall come upon me and overtake me, because I obey the voice of the Lord my God: Blessed shall I be in the city and blessed shall I be in the country. Blessed shall be the fruit of my body, the Producer of my ground and the increase of my herds, the increase of my cattle and the offspring of my flocks. Blessed shall be my basket and my kneading bowl. Blessed shall I be when I come in, and blessed shall I be when I go out. The Lord will cause my enemies who rise against me to be defeated before my face; they shall come out against me one way and flee before me in seven ways. The Lord will command the blessing on me in my storehouses and in all to which I set my hand, and He will bless me in the land which the Lord my God is giving me. The Lord will establish me as a holy people to Himself, just as He has sworn to me if I keep the commandments of the Lord my God and walk in His ways. Then all peoples of the earth shall see that I am called by the Name of the Lord, and they shall be afraid of me. And the Lord will grant me plenty of goods, in the fruit of my body, in the increase of my livestock, and in the produce of my ground, in the land of which the Lord swore to my fathers to give me. The Lord will open to me His good treasure, the heavens, to give the rain to my land in its season, and to bless all the work of my hand. I shall lend to many nations, but I shall not borrow. And the Lord will make me the head and not the tail; I shall be above only, and not be beneath if I heed to the commandments of the Lord my God, which He commands me today, and are careful to see them. So, I shall not turn aside from any of the words which He commands me this day; I will not move on to the right or to the left, I will not go after other gods."*

I pray this prayer in Jesus' Name.

Amen!

Six

THE JABEZ PRAYER

THE JABEZ PRAYER, "*JABEZ cried out to the God of Israel, "Oh that You would bless me and enlarge my territory! Let your hand be with me, and keep me from harm so that I will be free from pain."* And God granted his request" (1 Chronicles 4:10).

The Bible has many examples of prayers that teach us to depend on God and call upon Him. 1 Chronicles 4:10 tells us that, Jabez cried to the God of Israel. He not only recognizes God as the one and only God, but he also acknowledges that blessings come from God and God alone. Jabez was not just referring to physical land when asking God to enlarge his territory. However, Jabez was not simply speaking about wealth and prosperity but speaking of impacting the Kingdom of God. Jabez wanted a change; he wanted his spiritual territory to increase, to claim generations for the Lord of Israel. Jabez understood the power of God, "*Keep me from harm so that I will be free from pain.*" The name Jabez means *"pain."* His mother named him pain because of the pain she suffered during childbirth. When Jabez prays, he speaks against the testimony of his name and let's go of the shame it covered him in.

The Jabez Prayer:

Father, Your word is true, and You are not a man, that should lie, nor a son of man, that should repent. I stand boldly on the Word of God. I thank You, oh God, for the glory of the Lord is my salvation, the rock of my strength, and my refuge. I praise You, Father because You are worthy to be praised.

Father, in the Name of Jesus, give me the faith I need, Oh Lord, to believe these words as I pray the Jabez prayer. The Bible says, *"Jabez cried out to the God of Israel, oh that You would bless me and enlarge my territory."* I too cry out to the God of Israel, that You oh God will bless me and enlarge my territory. Keep your hand on me, and keep me from harm so that I will be free from pain. Father, I ask that You bless the works of my hands. According to 1 Chronicles 5:20, we are told that God answered the prayers of the people because they trusted in Him. I believe and trust in Your Mighty Name. Father, Your word says, in Philippians 4:6–7, *"Be anxious for nothing, but in everything by prayer and supplication, with thanksgiving, let your requests be made known to God; and the peace of God, which surpasses all understanding, will guard your hearts and minds through Christ Jesus."*

I decree and declare that I will be anxious for nothing. But in everything by prayer and supplication with thanksgiving, I will make my requests known to You. I declare that I walk in the peace of God that surpasses all understanding, and it will guard my heart and mind in Christ Jesus. Father, in the Name of Jesus, I bring my needs to You. Your word declares, that whatever I ask in Your Name, You will give to me. Right now! In the Name of Jesus, I ask for new territories, new opportunities, new relationships, new businesses, new contracts, new appointments, new career, new ministry, new day, new health and finance.

I wear a coat of many colors. I decree and declare that I walk in the favor of God and men, and I shall possess all the new land God has for me. I declare that every place where I set my foot will be mine. Father, You promise that You will give us land we did not labor for, and cities we did not build. I decree and declare that I am eating from vineyards and olive groves that I did not plant, in the Name of Jesus. Father arise by your mercy, and move me to the place which is *"flowing with milk and honey."* I declare that everything this season should bring to me must come forth, in the Name of Jesus.

I declare that I am not a grasshopper *(Numbers 13:33)*. I refuse to worry or fear. Therefore, I bind the spirit of worry, fear, doubt, discouragement, and unbelief. I decree and declare the blessings of the Lord make me rich, and He adds no sorrow with it (Proverbs 10:22).

I am crowned with God's love and mercy and with all good things. I release the spirit of Jabez. I decree new territories. I decree and declare that I walk in faith and walk with my head high with humility. I pray for abundance, overflow, and for more than enough in the Name of Jesus.

I thank You, Father, for divine connections. Thank you for Your wisdom, knowledge, and understanding. Father God, open doors that no man has the power to close. I glorify You in all I do. In the Name of Jesus. I seal these prayers under the Blood of Jesus Christ!

Amen!

SEVEN

PRAYER FOR MARRIAGE RESTORATION

"Marriage is the greatest test in the world... but now I welcome the test instead of dreading it. It is much more than a test of the sweetness of temper, as people sometimes think; it is a test of the whole character and affects every action."

—T.S. Eliot

MY HUSBAND LEFT ME to live with another woman for six months. My heart was full of agony and pain, and my heart was broken. I felt empty inside. I was broken and hopeless. I just wanted to throw in the towel and wave the white flag. My marriage is over! What a painful thought. Meanwhile, I am reminded that God's *rod and staff, comforted me*. He alone, by His grace, snatched me from despair and brought me into His marvelous light. He taught me to trust Him irrevocably.

Needless to say, the loneliness of six months was excruciating and painfully long. But God! He was omnipresent through the process. My daily and intimate prayers with God made a clear pathway out of darkness. Yes, God defined the purpose of our marriage and kindled a newfound love for us. I then realized that God took me on an independent and spiritual journey, which birthed a higher level of faith and a newfound of sole dependence on God.

At that moment, with "all the authority that has been given to me in Heaven and the earth …" I declared war on the kingdom of darkness and battled in the spiritual realm. Prayer became my shield, the Word of God became my sword, and I cut down my enemy on all sides and all fronts each day. Every single day, my strength was the Word of God! He was my trainer, and I was His student. God trained my hands for war and my fingers for battle (Psalm 144:1). Once, I allowed the Holy Spirit to intervene in my mind and heart; I removed my butt out of the way. Yes, I finally released the wheel and let go. I let it all go—the worry, doubt, and accusations were all gone.

Through the process, at times, daunting and sleepless nights, I asked God to help me focus on Him more, and He did! After six months in God's presence, my husband came back to me. At the finish line, I gained the authority to move by faith—not by sight, and to truly trust God with all my heart, all my soul, all my mind, and all my strength. God is faithful! Praise Report: My husband returned home into a transformed man of God; his mind was renewed; he had an unexplainable hunger for God's Word with a deep desire to serve God.

Prayer for Marriage Restoration/ Wife and Husband

Father, in the Name of Jesus, I give You all the glory and all the praise that is due to Your great name. I thank You in advance for answering my prayer concerning my spouse and me. Father, I lift up my spouse before you. I bind all satanic forces that would try to come against my spouse and me, in the Name of Jesus Christ.

I declare and decree that I am being molded to be the great husband/wife that You call me to be. Father, right now, in the Name of Jesus Christ, I release the anointing of the Holy Spirit to bind every ungodly soul tie. I break and destroy every assignment and attack of the enemy. Father, You have given us the authority in Mathew 16:19 to bind and loose in heaven and on earth. With the authority that has been given to me, I bind everything that hinders me, from fulfilling Your perfect plans in my marriage.

I decree and declare in the Mighty Name of Jesus, every spirit of fornication, adultery, disrespect, lack of intimacy, unforgiveness, bitterness, resentment, anger, the evil spirit of Jezebel, the spirit of divorce, spirit of separation, verbal and physical abuse, substance abuse, evil speaking, slander, lack of communication, bad temper, rejection, broken-heartedness, homosexuality, pornography, bad habits, indignation, pride, as well as all types of evil behavior, is loosed, broken, and removed off my marriage in the Mighty Name of Jesus.

Father God, You are all-powerful and all-knowing, You can mend any bridges that may have been burned by conflict, clear away any confusion, and give us the power we need to forgive one and other. I decree and declare that I stand firm in faith that my marriage is resurrected from the dead by the hands of the Holy Spirit. Therefore, I speak healing over my marriage. Father, I ask that you restore our first love, the love we once had for one another. Father, I ask that You restore my marriage to be a testimony to Your glory. I speak love, tenderheartedness, forgiveness, peace, honesty, patience, trust, respect, intimacy, passion, oneness, laughter, harmony, companionship, rekindling passion, understanding, closeness, faithfulness, fellowship, submission, stability, self-control, friendship, unity, fun, and supernatural joy into my marriage in the Name of Jesus.

By faith in the Name of Jesus, I declare that our marriage is restored. Father Your word says, *"What God has joined together, let not man separate."* Therefore, I put the full armor of God on myself and my spouse so that we can stand against the devil's schemes.

I declare, in the Name of Jesus, we will experience God's faithfulness. We will not worry. We will not doubt. We will keep trusting in You, oh God, knowing that You will not fail us. We hide our marriage under the Blood of Jesus, in Jesus' Mighty name! We pray this prayer with confidence in Jesus' Name.

I seal this prayer in the Name of Jesus.

Amen!

EIGHT

MARRIAGE PRAYER

EPHESIANS 5:21-28, *"SUBMIT TO one another out of reverence for Christ. Wives, submit yourselves to your own husbands as you do to the Lord. For the husband is the head of the wife as Christ is the head of the church, his body, of which he is the Savior. Now as the church submits to Christ, so also wives should submit to their husbands in everything. Husbands, love your wives, just as Christ loved the church and gave himself up for her to make her holy, cleansing her by the washing with water through the word, and to present her to himself as a radiant church, without stain or wrinkle or any other blemish, but holy and blameless. In this same way, husbands ought to love their wives as their own bodies. He who loves his wife loves himself."*

* * *

Marriage is an honorable thing and was designed and instituted by God. Everything that God created, He declared it was good. Consequently, so it is with this wonderful union called marriage. Hebrews 13:4 says, *"Marriage should be honored by all, and the marriage bed kept pure, for God will judge the adulterer and all the sexually immoral."*

What God desires and has always desired is to take two people and seam them together to intertwine them holistically with Him embedded in the relationship. Mark 10:8 states, *"And the two will become one flesh. So they are no longer two, but one flesh."* He has already given us the tools we need to fulfill all He has called us to do. Marriage is under attack because it is something good. It is always a wonderful thing when two people are willing to love and cherish each other regardless of their differences. Satan does not want us to succeed in our marriages, so he attacks our marriages in many ways. Our job is to stay in prayer and not give the enemy any room to enter. 1 Peter 5:8 states it vividly, *"Be alert and of sober mind. Your enemy the devil prowls around like a roaring lion looking for someone to devour."*

Praying for your marriage is indispensable if you want to have a blossoming relationship and to see God's power in your marriage. Commit to prayer together. Devote yourselves to it. Carve out time to pray because it is the only power you have over your enemy. God will speak to you regularly if you abide in him. When you and your spouse are committed to abiding in him, you will ensure that nothing gets in your way. You are never too busy to do something if it is your priority. If your commitment to prayer and desire to abide in Christ is a priority for you, you will do it. That is the bottom line.

Instead of saying, "We didn't have time to pray," say instead that "It was not a priority for us to pray today." It leaves a bitter taste in your mouth, doesn't it? It is true though, isn't it? You have plenty of time to do the things that matter the most to you. You had plenty of time to go to work and earn a living. You had plenty of time to buy or cook your meals, and you had plenty of time for social media. Those priorities are essential, yes. However, prayer is crucial. If you are starving, you will put everything else on hold until after you eat. If you want victory over the Devil, you absolutely *must* pray together. Ecclesiastes eloquently states, *"Two are better than one because they have a more satisfying return for their labor; for if either of them falls, then one will lift up his companion. But woe to him who is alone when he falls and does not have another to lift him up. Again, if two lie down together, then they keep warm; but how can one be warm alone? And though one can overpower him who is alone, two can resist him. A cord of three strands is not quickly broken" (Ecclesiastes 4:9–12)*. Don't relegate it to a corner of your life and then wonder why the Devil is constantly attacking your marriage—you are letting him!

Thus, put on your armor and start fighting. It is time to stop allowing the Devil to have access to your marriage. It is time to cease to be a victim of his attacks and his lies. It is time to stand up and enforce the victory

Christ already won for you. Satan knows he has been defeated and he knows that you know it too, but as much time as you just lie there and do nothing to prevent him from attacking your relationship, he is going to take advantage of your unawareness, pride, and laziness and lay siege to your marriage. It is high time for you and your spouse to rise and gird yourselves. Speak out the truth and the Word of God against any and every attack. Set your boundaries and claim your territory. Be actively employed on the offensive so that the enemy gets no chance to come anywhere near your marriage.

Praying for Your Marriage

Father in the Name of Jesus, I give You all the glory, all the honor, and all the praise. You are worthy to be praised. There is truly nobody like You. I praise You oh God for Your loving-kindness, and for Your tender mercy. I trust in You, oh God with all my heart and all my soul. For Your word says, *"Where two or three are gathered together in your name, there you are in the midst."*

I declare and decree that my marriage is ordained by God the Creator. I declare that we are one, we walk in unity and agreement in our body, mind, soul, and spirit. I take authority against anything that is a hindrance or stumbling block in my marriage; I release the power of the Holy Ghost to work in both myself and my spouse's life. Father, your word declares, *"If we agree on earth concerning anything, it will be done."* I stand in agreement with the Word of God concerning my marriage. I declare and decree that there is no lack in our marriage. We will live faithfully and lovingly together in Jesus' Name.

I release angels on assignment, to guide, protect, and deliver us from any temptation. I anoint my marriage with the Blood of Jesus. I loose the Spirit of love, joy, peace, patience, kindness, goodness, faithfulness, gentleness, and self-control over my spouse and me. We put the Lord Jesus as a garment. We put on the breastplate of faith and love. We put on the helmet of salvation. We put on the armor of light. We bind mercy and truth around our neck, we write them on the tablet of our heart. We win favor and a good name in the sight of God and man. By faith, we walk like Kings and Queens, we talk like Kings and Queens, we think like Kings and Queens, we dress like Kings and Queens.

I declare and decree that no weapon formed against our marriage will be able to prosper. Right now, in the name of Jesus, I decree and declare that the bondage of lies, ignorance, strongholds, and deception are broken off my spouse in Jesus' Name. I reverse every assignment, evil plan or attack against my spouse and me from Satan and his angels, and I send them back 7 times in the Name of Jesus. I stand against the spirit of adultery, the spirit of anger, jealousy, unforgiveness, confusion, resentment, division, extreme competition, in the Name of Jesus. I come against every negative word that was spoken to cause problems in my marriage, whether through my spouse or me, I reverse them in the Name of Jesus.

I declare in the name of Jesus, no man, no woman, no demon, and no stronghold will separate what God has joined together. I stand on the Word, what God has joined together let no one come between. I declare that our marriage is covered under the Blood of Jesus Christ, our home, our family, our children, and all that we have are covered under the Blood of Jesus.

I pray these things with complete confidence. Nevertheless, not my will, but thine will be done.

Amen!

NINE

PRAYERS FOR THE UNWED

Singleness can be a long, lonely, and confusing road, especially when it's unwanted.

—Anonymous

OUR PRAYER SHOULD ALWAYS be, *"Not my will, Lord, but yours be done"* (Luke 22:42). It is a hard prayer to pray when all you want is someone to share your life with, someone to walk this journey with you. The prayer mentioned above means surrendering your ideals, hopes, wants and yes, even your timetable to God to do as He wants. Maybe He will ask you to wait on Him for another decade or maybe just another hour. Maybe He will ask you to die to yourself so that you can be molded into the spouse you need to be before you meet the one for you.

Marriage is a journey, and much of it requires that we chisel parts of ourselves off or shape it into another form for the benefit of our spouse and our marriage. Ask the Lord to prepare you for your marriage and your future spouse, and to give you a heart of grace, love, and forgiveness so that you can work through the internal and external situation. Ask God to prepare your spouse for marriage to you as well. Begin your search for your spouse in God's heart and ask Him to lead you to your spouse. If you rely on God for direction and confirmation, you will never go wrong. You are asking for a *"good thing."* Pray for wisdom and discernment so that when they enter your life, your spirit will already be lined up with what you asked for.

Get wisdom! Get understanding! Do not forget, nor turn away from the words of my mouth. Do not forsake her, and she will preserve you: love her, and she will keep you. Wisdom is the principal thing; therefore, get wisdom. And in all your getting, get understanding (Proverbs 4:5–7). God has instructed us to come to Him for wisdom. James 1:5 promises, *"If any of you lacks wisdom, let him ask of God, who gives to all liberally and without reproach, and it will be given to him."*

Prayer for the Unwed:

Father in the Name of Jesus, according to Genesis 2:18, You said, *"It is not good for the man to be alone. You will make a helper suitable for him."* Therefore, it is Your plan that I have a helpmate. It is Your desire that I not be alone, so as You took the time to prepare Adam for the arrival of his mate, I pray that I too will go through the preparation process with patience and godly endurance.

I decree and declare that I am not incomplete, but I am whole person. I do not need another to complete me, for I am in Christ, and Christ is in me. I declare that I will enter marriage whenever it is suitable for you. I pray for patience to reign in my life as I wait for You to hand-pick my future spouse. As King Solomon declared, the man who finds a wife, finds a good thing. I declare that my eyes and the eyes of my future spouse will be open that we will recognize each other when the time comes. I pray for clarity of thought that love will blind neither I nor my future spouse.

Every spirit that has caused my spouse not to see me, I curse now with the Blood of Jesus. There will be no delay, no hindrances, no distractions.

Father, I decree and declare that I will receive my godly spouse. My marriage is already ordained in the heavenly realms because I have all spiritual blessings in heavenly places. It's already done. It's already mine. I claim and receive my godly spouse in the Name of Jesus.

Father, I believe you have created me for a special person, and I declare in the Name of Jesus that my future spouse will find me. I pray, as I wait for my mate, that You help me stay focused on You. I will not cease thanking You for my godly spouse. Father of glory, bless me with the spirit of wisdom and revelation in the knowledge of You that I may be able to recognize when you send people into my life. Open the eyes of my understanding, that I will know the hope of Your calling and what the riches of the glory of Your inheritance is in the saints; that I may experience Your exceeding great power through faith in Christ. This I pray and also declare for my future spouse. May we never wander from Your commandments but meditate on Your precepts and respect Your ways that You will guide our steps according to Your Words, plans, and purposes for our lives, that as we walk in Your ways, Your path will also lead us to each other, in Jesus Name. (Read Ephesians 1:16–19 and Psalm 119:10, 15, 37, 133)

According to Lamentations 3:25–26, "*It is good for those who hope and wait quietly for Your salvation.*" I declare, while I am waiting patiently, that You would guard my heart and mind with the assurance of Jeremiah 29:11, for You, Lord, know the thoughts You think towards me thoughts of peace, and not of evil, to give me an expected end.

TEN

EARLY MORNING PRAYER

IF YOU ARE A budding prayer warrior, you will soon discover what the seasoned warriors already know: it is a discipline. Prayer warriors do not just pray only when they "feel like it." They discipline themselves and their lives to make prayer a priority. Life will happen, and it can be easy to put prayer to the side or make it something you hurriedly tick off your list at the end or beginning of your day. That will not work if you desire to have an empowered, productive, and victorious prayer life. You must make time for it, whether that means getting up earlier, sleeping later or cutting your lunch hour in half. As you grow, it will become more natural to "pray without ceasing" but for now, focus on trying to "pray without sleeping."

All you need is your Sword (your Bible) and your heart. (You might also want something to write notes on as the Spirit ministers to you from the Word and during prayer). Set up a corner of the room in your home as your prayer closet. If you cannot dedicate a prayer space, then have a basket that holds your supplies and a mat that you can roll out when you pray to divide the space and make it portable to wherever the new, quiet spot may be in your house (even if it is the bathroom).

If you cannot find time during your day, then sacrifice a little sleep to wake up earlier or go to bed later while everyone else is asleep. Use the serendipity peace to still your heart and talk to your Father.

A life of prayer, as already stated, is a life of discipline. Do it when you are not motivated to and be honest with God that you are not motivated to pray but that you still want to develop a prayer life. He already knows how you feel and He understands. The effort is pleasing to Him, and you may just find that your lack of motivation becomes a deeper desire to press into God more as the Spirit ministers to your heart and blesses you because your heart is in the right place.

As you discipline yourself early in the morning, you will find that it soon becomes automatic for you to pray without ceasing and to rejoice continually in the Lord because you become used to relying on the Lord for every need and desire. Make time for prayer every morning, and you will soon be a life-long prayer warrior. It will become a habit and a lifestyle in no time at all.

Early Morning Prayer:

"I lay down and slept; I awoke, for the Lord sustained me"

(Psalm 3:5). Father in the Name of Jesus, I bless and glorify Your Name. I thank You for waking me up this morning to embrace the sunlight that comes down from the heavens. I thank You for covering my family and me under the precious Blood of Jesus. Thank You for giving Your angels charge over us, to guard us wherever we may go. Father, wash and purify us from the crown of our head to the sole of our feet. Cleanse me oh Lord from all sin and unrighteousness. Your word says in Romans 10:13 *"Everyone who calls on the name of the Lord will be saved."* I call on Your Name this morning Father, for You can save me from the plans and schemes of the enemy. I surrender myself completely to You and You alone.

I decree and declare, *"This is the day the Lord has made; we will rejoice and be glad in it"* (Psalm 118:24). Father God, in the Name of Jesus, I take authority and claim my victory over my enemies this morning. I plead the blood of Jesus over every principality, power, ruler of darkness, and spiritual wickedness in high places assigned to destroy my purpose and my calling. I bind every evil spirit and every evil plan of the enemy that is made to frustrate and hinder me today. Satan! I rebuke you, and I command you, in the Name of Jesus to leave my presence, and go back to the pit of hell where you belong.

According to Colossians 1:13, we have been delivered from the authority of darkness and placed into God's kingdom. Father Your words say in Matthew 28:18–19 *"All authority has been given to Me in heaven and on earth."*

Therefore, in the Name of Jesus, I take authority over the kingdom of darkness, and I destroy the power of all demonic forces. With the Blood of Jesus, and the authority that has been given to me, I bind up every demon that was sent to follow me today back to SENDER!

I call forth legions of warrior angel to battle on my behalf. I break, destroy, bind, block, knock down every witch, warlock, off their thrones this morning. I release angels on assignment, I assign them, to my home, my workplace, my ministry, my business, in the Name of Jesus. I decree and declare that I am covered and protected by the Blood of Jesus Christ. I place a hedge of fire around myself and my loved ones. Spirit of the living God, come from the four winds of the earth and turn me into a great warrior for Your glory. I prophesy as He commanded me, in the Name of Jesus Christ today is the day that all my dreams are coming to pass. Father God, You are faithful to Your words. All Your promises are *"Yes" and "Amen."* Therefore, today in the Name of Jesus, I turn all "No" into "Yes" in the Name of Jesus. I declare *"that all things are working together for my good according to His purpose."* I have purpose in this hour. I have purpose in this season. According to Ecclesiastes 3:1, *"To everything there is a season, and a time to every purpose under the heaven."* I declare it is my NOW time and my NOW season. I decree and declare I am one of a kind. I am His masterpiece, His most prized possession. I walk with my head held high today, knowing that I am the child of the

Most High God. I declare that everything concerning me today is already lined up for His glory. No one, no sickness, no disappointment, can stop God's plan over my life. What He promised will come to pass because His Word says, *"God is not a man, that he should lie; neither the son of man, that he should repent."*

I seal this prayer in the Name of Jesus.

Amen!

ELEVEN

MIDNIGHT WARFARE PRAYER

PAUL AND SILAS HAD a plan that did wonders. In the midst of their darkest moment, they were stripped, beaten with rods, and thrown into prison. When everyone else was asleep, and all things were dark; they prayed doubtlessly for God to deliver them.

> *"But at midnight Paul and Silas were praying and singing hymns to God, and the prisoners were listening to them. Suddenly there was a great earthquake, so that the foundations of the prison were shaken; and immediately all the doors were opened, and everyone's chains were loosed."*
>
> ACTS 16:25–26

David knew the significance of midnight prayers. He says, *"At midnight I will rise to give thanks to You, because of Your righteous judgments"* (Psalm 119:62).

Be faithful to pray every night. Train yourself to pray

at that midnight hour. Think of it like you are conducting your rounds as a watchman. Every time you pray, even if it is five minutes, you are making a round on your property to ensure that it is protected from the enemy.

Midnight Warfare Prayer

Father God, I come before You in the Name of Jesus. *"You are the God that answers by fire"* (1 Kings 18:24). You are the consuming fire. Heaven and earth are full of Your presence and glory. Father, I ask that You consume in me those things which must be burnt as I advance in this prayer.

I decree and declare I have tongues of fire, therefore, I call forth the Fire of the Holy Ghost to destroy the works of the devil. I declare that the evil works of the devil are destroyed. I release the Fire of God to burn up the works of darkness. According to Psalm 17:6–8, *"If I call on You, my God, You will answer me; You will turn Your ear to me and hear my prayer, You will show me the wonders of Your great love, You who save by Your right hand those who take refuge in You from their foes. Keep me as the apple of Your eye, and hide me in the shadow of Your wings."* Father, the Bible declares, as Paul and Silas prayed and sang praises to Your Name, Your Spirit shook the whole prison chamber, and there was a great earthquake, the foundations of the prison were shaken: and immediately all the doors were opened, and everyone was set free. I decree and declare that the Spirit of God will move at midnight to set the captives free in the Name of Jesus. I decree and declare that doors are opened, channels opened, no man, no devil, and no spirit can shut the door that God has opened unto me. I declare that I will walk through all doors that the Lord has opened to me.

Your word declares in Mark 13:33–35, *"Take heed, keep on the alert; for you do not know when the appointed time will come. It is like a man away on a journey, who upon leaving his house and putting his slaves in charge, assigning to each one his task, also commanded the doorkeeper to stay on the alert. Therefore, be on the alert—for you do not know when the master of the house is coming, whether in the evening, at midnight, or when the rooster crows, or in the morning."* I declare whenever our Lord comes; He will not find us sleeping. We will be preparing to meet Him in the Name of Jesus.

Father, You have given me the authority to trample on snakes and scorpions and to overcome all the power of the enemy; nothing will harm me (Luke 10:19). I decree and declare, *"A thousand may fall at my side, and ten thousand at my right; it shall not come near me."* I declare war against the plans of the enemy. I declare and decree Fire of the Holy Ghost! I bind and rebuke the spirit of Jezebel, Ahab, the powers of Pharaoh and every satanic bondage and limitations that hinder me from praying at midnight in the Name of Jesus.

I sprinkle the Blood of Jesus over my loved ones and

me. We put on the armor of light. We are victorious. We receive fresh fire in the Name of Jesus.

I seal this prayer in the Name of Jesus.

Amen!

Twelve

A PRAYER OF REPENTANCE

SATAN HAS LEGAL AUTHORITY over you when you sin. Even if you have been saved, if you sin, you have given Satan legal rights to work in your life (Romans 7: 22–25). Until you confess your sin, he can stay in your life. But, the moment that you confess your sin and ask forgiveness, Jesus forgives you and then—only then—do you have the authority from Jesus to command Satan to leave because you have just broken his claim to authority over your life. Then, he must listen to you because your sins have been forgiven.

Repentance preceded every revival in the Scripture. Before Gabriel visited Daniel, he repented for his sins and the sins of his people (Daniel 9). Before revival broke out in the nation of Israel after they returned from captivity, Ezra and the people renounced and turned away from their sins (Ezra 9–10). God wanted to work in the lives of His people and return to the nation but so long as their unconfessed sins stood in the way, He could not.

But as soon as they repented, that separation was torn away, and God's glory and power were made evident in their midst.

While you have unconfessed sin in your life, you can command the devil to do what you want him to do until you're blue in the face, but it will not do you any good because you have granted him authority over your life. But the minute you turn that sin over to Jesus, acknowledge that you have sinned and have rebelled against God and ask forgiveness, you will be forgiven (1 John 1:9). At that moment, that sin has no authority over you, and with that, Satan's authority over you is broken as well.

Everyone who is saved by the blood of the Lamb has been given authority by Jesus to live victorious life, but he or she must ensure that they continually abide in Him (John 15:4). This is a vital principle in prayer. Just as the branch that separates from the tree withers and dies, so too will you die if you try to operate on your own. You have been grafted to Jesus, and apart from Him, you cannot do anything. With him though, you can reign over all circumstance, especially the heart-wrenching ones.

A Prayer of Repentance:

Father, I acknowledge my sin, and I also acknowledge Your capacity and willingness to truly forgive me on the merit of Jesus' sacrifice on the Cross. Jesus Christ paid my debt in full by His suffering and His sacrifice. He gave His body, and every drop of His blood for my salvation and redemption and it is through His blood that I can access full atonement for my sins; past, present, and future. I repent of my sins, and I turn to You for healing and restoration.

Father, Your word makes it clear that if I repent, humble myself, turn from my evil ways and pray, that I would experience Your power in every area of my life. There is no sin that I desire to hide from You, Abba, for I seek to dwell perpetually in Your presence. There is no sin that I wish to cling to at the cost of losing Your manifested glory in my life. Even those that are hidden, those sins of omission that I may fail to recognize as sin, I confess them all to You.

I confess my deeds and thoughts that are rooted in my fallenness. I confess my bad attitude to You and towards others; my failure to love You with all my heart, mind, and soul and to love others above myself, which fulfills the commandments. I confess my incapacity to walk in perfection by my own strength and efforts, and in repenting this day, I also admit my desperate need for You in every area of my life. You are my perfection and my righteousness, for my own righteousness is nothing but filthy rags.

Father, I claim Your forgiveness. You said, if we repent, You are faithful and ready to forgive. You said, I am forgiven as I forgive others. Therefore, in seeking Your forgiveness Father, I also choose to forgive those who have offended and hurt me. I choose to forgive those who speak death over me. And I ask You to forgive me, for I am also guilty of these sins. I ask for mercy, Father, for my flesh cannot bear the judgment of my own sins, in Jesus Name.

In the Name of Jesus, according to Psalm 103:2–5, I thank you for removing all my iniquities, for healing all my diseases, for redeeming my life from destruction, and for crowning me with Your loving-kindness and tender mercies. Father, in the Name of Jesus, Your word says in Jeremiah 24:6–7, that You will set Your eyes on me, and You will bring me back. You will build me up, and not tear me down; You will plant me, and not pluck me up. You will give me the heart to know that You are the LORD my God, and I shall be your child, and You will be my God, for I shall return to You with my whole heart.

I decree and declare that I am forgiven; therefore, I am justified by faith, and I am now qualified to walk in the newness of life, In Jesus Name. Amen.

A Personal Prayer of Repentance from Psalm 51:

I thank you, Father, I give You glory, I give You honor, and I give You praise. Father in the Name of Jesus I decree and declare as I come to Your throne boldly with the Blood of Jesus, I ask that You Have mercy on me, O God, according to Your lovingkindness; according to the greatness of Your compassion blot out my transgressions.

Wash me thoroughly from my wickedness and guilt. And cleanse me from my sin. For I am conscious of my transgressions, and I acknowledge them; my sin is always before me. Against You, You only, have I sinned and done that which is evil in Your sight so that You are justified when You speak [Your sentence]. And faultless in Your judgment. I was brought forth in [a state of] wickedness; in sin, my mother conceived me [and from my beginning I, too, was sinful]. Behold, You desire truth in the innermost being, and in the hidden part [of my heart] You will make me know wisdom. Purify me with [a] hyssop, and I will be clean; wash me, and I will be whiter than snow. Make me hear joy and gladness and be satisfied; let the bones which You have broken rejoice. Hide Your face from my sins. And blot out all my iniquities. Create in me a clean heart, O God, and renew a right and steadfast spirit within me. Do not cast me away from Your presence. And do not take Your Holy Spirit from me. Restore to me the joy of Your salvation. And sustain me with a willing spirit. Then I will teach transgressors Your ways, and sinners shall be converted and return to You. Rescue me from bloodguiltiness, O God, the God of my salvation; then my tongue will sing joyfully of Your righteousness and Your justice. O Lord, open my lips, that my mouth may declare Your praise.

THIRTEEN

BREAKING GENERATIONAL CURSES

"You shall not bow down to [idols] or worship them; for I, the Lord your God, am a jealous God, punishing the children for the sin of the fathers to the third and fourth generation of those who hate me."

EXODUS 20:5

GENERATIONAL CURSES CAN PLAGUE a person without their knowledge. The one and the only way to break a generational curse or any curse for that matter is to "make it obedient to Christ." That is, to take the sin that caused the curse and repent of it. Repent before God's presence for your own sins that are attributed to the curse and repent for your forefathers, just as Daniel did.

God is faithful and just to forgive us when we ask, so you can be sure you have been forgiven. However, the enemy does not abide by laws of God so even though you have been forgiven, you must be vigilant to guard yourself against the temptation to sin in the same manner that brought the curse on your family. Forgive your forefathers and realize that you are not responsible for their actions. You have asked forgiveness for yourself to break the curse and God will honor that, but it is their responsibility to do the same for their own sins.

Prayer for Breaking Generational Curses

Father, today I come in the name of the resurrected Jesus Christ, that at the Name of Jesus every knee shall bow, in heaven, on earth, and under the earth, and that every tongue shall confess that Jesus Christ is Lord. You are the Almighty Father, the Creator of the heaven and earth. You are the Christ, who died for me so that I may live. Father, I bless your Name, truly you are worthy to be praised. I ask that you forgive myself, and my family for our sins; going back four generations. Wash us from the crown of our head to the sole of our feet. I declare we are cleansed with the blood of Jesus.

I declare that we are more than a conqueror (Romans 8:37), everything we touch shall be blessed. I declare supernatural increase, supernatural miracle, favor, wealth, riches, power, and influence in our family in the Name of Jesus. We are favorable in the sight of God, and men. Father, as you clothed the children of

Israel with favor, we too are clothed with the favor of God in the Name of Jesus! I declare that we are wearing a coat of many colors.

Father in the Name of Jesus, I decree and declare that I am set free from all generational curses brought by the sins of my forefathers. Your Word declares in Romans 2:5–6, "*You will render to every man according to his deeds, for we shall all stand before the judgment seat and every one of us shall give an account of himself to God.*" Any trace of generational curses in my blood-line, I replace it with generational blessings. I declare we are blessed, prosperous, healthy, sober, free and happy in the Name of Jesus. I release the blessing of the Lord over my family. I declare we are Abraham's seeds, we are blessed in the city, we are blessed in the field. I declare that we are the children of the King! We are clothed with godly strength and dignity! We are loved! I declare that we are blessed not cursed. We are the head, not the tail. We are rich, not poor. We are healed, not sick. I declare we are free! We receive freedom and peace today because our mind has been renewed.

I rebuke all the dysfunctional habits and curses that have been passed down to me from my parents, grandparents, great-grandparents, and other family members in the Name of Jesus. I decree and declare that no weapon formed against me shall prosper, therefore, I put on the armor of light. By the Blood of Jesus Christ, I declare that Satan has no authority and no power over me and my loved ones. I break and destroy the curse of divorce, fornication, and adultery in my family. I come against and take authority over every witchcraft, palm reading, alcoholism, verbal or physical abuse, drugs, mental illness, physical diseases, sexual molestation, homosexuality, masturbation, depression, poverty, low self-esteem, pornography, greed, jealousy, laziness, violence, murder, lying, and lust and say they are broken and lifted off my family in Jesus' Name.

No weapon of Satan and his agents formed against us shall prosper, in the Name of Jesus. I bind all ungodly spirit of rejection, distraction, isolation, death, violence, insecurity, peer pressure, and every other evil spirit working against our destiny in Jesus' Name. I declare that every chain that has held my family captive and in bondage is broken in the Name of Jesus. I go back four generations and cancel every curse and demons that have been passed down to destroy our family. We break the stronghold of Satan and command him to flee, in the Name of Jesus.

I declare that we are in right standing with God and that our bodies are the temple of the Holy Spirit. According to Galatians 3:13–14, *"We have been redeemed from the curse of the law, (for it is written, "Cursed is everyone who hangs on a tree", that the blessing of Abraham might come upon the Gentiles in Christ Jesus, that we might receive the promise of the Spirit through faith."* Father, we thank you for saving us from the kingdom of darkness and bringing us into your marvelous light.

I seal this prayer in the Name of Jesus

Amen!

FOURTEEN

PRAYER FOR MINISTRY

"In everything set them an example by doing what is good. In your teaching show integrity, seriousness and soundness of speech that cannot be condemned…"

TITUS 2:7–8

REGARDLESS OF WHO YOU are and what you do, you have a ministry and a purpose. The people in your life are a part of it for a reason. They could be the sweetest people in the world or your worst enemies but you, a Christian, a representative and ambassador of the King, are part of their lives for a specific purpose. Once you begin to see your life and filter every day—and each interaction with any person—through this perspective, everything changes. You may be the only Jesus people see. What kind of Jesus are you portraying? You may be the only representation of unconditional love a person experiences, what kind of love are you sharing? *"Whatever* *happens, conduct yourselves in a manner worthy of the gospel of Christ."* (Phil 1:27.)

Thus says the Lord God to the shepherds: "Woe to the shepherds of Israel who feed themselves! Should not the shepherds feed the flocks? You eat the fat and clothe yourselves with the wool; you slaughter the fatlings, but you do not feed the flock. The weak you have not strengthened, nor have you healed those who were sick, nor bound up the broken, nor brought back what was driven away, nor sought what was lost; but with force and cruelty you have ruled them. So they were scattered because there was no shepherd; and they became food for all the beasts of the field when they were scattered" (Ezekiel 34:1–5).

You are important, and your ministry is important. You have a purpose. You may never stand on a stage and witness to a million people, but you still have a ministry. You may never physically lead someone to Christ, but their life will be impacted—for better or worse—through the way you depict God at home, at work, in the store or even on the street. One day, in eternity, you will see the fruit of your labor or lack thereof. What will your testimony be when you stand before men? What will your testimony be when you stand before the King of kings?

Prayer for Ministry:

Father, in the Name of Jesus, I thank you for Your wisdom, guidance, and anointing. I thank You for anointing me and for counting me faithful to do the ministry work you call me to do. Thank You, Father, for filling and empowering me to be an effective minister for Your glory.

Father, Your Word declares, *"You are the head of the body, the church, who is the beginning, the firstborn from the dead, that in all things You may have the preeminence."* Father, You are the Creator and Sustainer of all things. I pray that whatever I do, I do it heartily, as to You, and not to men, because I know my reward comes from only You.

I decree and declare that I am an example of Jesus Christ, who came to earth not to be served, but to serve others and give His life as a ransom for many (Matthew 20:28). Father build us up in the unity of the Holy Spirit and may we be transformed into the likeness of Jesus Christ by the renewing of our mind. I declare that God's grace shall equip me to let my light shine before others so that they may see the good works and give glory to the Father who is in heaven (Matthew 5:16). I declare that I am clothed with a double portion of God's anointing. Father in the Name of Jesus, guide us, anoint us that we may go into all the world and preach the gospel to everyone (Mark 16:15). I declare they will know us by our fruits.

I release the love of God. I release signs and wonders and supernatural blessings into my ministry. We release the Word of God, the spirit of prayer, and fasting into our ministry in the Name of Jesus. We release ourselves from every stronghold of the enemy which bombards our minds, hearts, and thoughts. Father, in the Name of

Jesus, as we stand in unity to do Your work, we break and destroy every stronghold of the enemy by the Word of the Holy Ghost.

Father, Your Word promises, *"If anyone thirsts, let him come to You and drink. He who believes in You, as the Scripture has said, out of his heart will flow rivers of living water"* (John 7:37–39). I declare that the river of living water is pouring out of me. I release fresh anointing and fresh oil upon the ministry of my Church. We take authority over the spirits of doubt, fear, pride, envy, temptation, jealousy, and competition. We put on the whole armor of God. We put on righteousness as a breastplate, the helmet of salvation on our head; we put on the garments of praise and wrap ourselves in zeal.

I declare that the anointing of God breaks and destroys every yoke in my ministry. I decree we are trail-blazers, and I release apostolic and prophetic anointing into my ministry. I declare that, *"The Spirit of the Lord that is upon us, will anoint us to preach the gospel to the poor; to heal the brokenhearted, to proclaim liberty to the captives and recovery of sight to the blind, to set at liberty those who are oppressed"* (Luke 4:18). I decree and declare "The fire shall always be burning on the altar, it shall never go out" (Leviticus 6:13). I decree and declare that the fire of evangelism will begin to burn in the heart of the people. I release fresh fire, fresh winds, fresh oil, and new revelation upon the people in my church.

According to Isaiah 40:31, they that wait upon the

LORD shall renew their strength; they shall mount up with wings as eagles; they shall run, and not be weary; and they shall walk, and not faint. I plead the Blood of Jesus over my spiritual senses. I declare, in this season, we will wait on the LORD and soar like eagles. I declare we have eagle eyes. We have 20/20 vision in the spirit. I speak to my spiritual eyes; I command the layers of tissue of our eyes to be filled with the Blood of Jesus that we may be able to see our desire and the desire of our enemies. Father open our eyes and ears to see and hear the things of the Spirit.

For it is written, the Lord is our Shepherd, and we shall have no lack. I declare every dark covenant that has been set against the call of God on my life is destroyed in the Name of Jesus. I shall walk, talk, look, and sound like Christ. I declare nothing, and no one will hinder the work that I must do for my God. I am appointed and anointed to preach the good news to the nation.

I seal this prayer in the Name of Jesus.
Amen!

Fifteen

PRAYER FOR YOUR CHILDREN

"I have no greater joy than to hear that my children are walking in the truth."

3 John 1:4

ONE OF THE MOST frightening realities any parent has to deal with is that we cannot protect our children from all the dangers in the world around us. We hear about heart-wrenching tragedies, and we wish with all our hearts to scoop up our children and protect them from all harm.

While we cannot hide our children, we can pray for them. We can guard them through intercession. We can pray for wisdom to teach them so that they can make their own decisions wisely. We can pray that they may be protected while they are away from us. We can pray that their hearts may seek the Lord and love Him with all their soul, mind, and might.

We can also pray that God's will be done in their

lives even if it does not necessarily line up with our own hopes and dreams for them. We can pray for them to turn back to the Lord and to us when they choose to sin, choose to walk away from us or choose to walk away from the Lord.

In all our prayers though, there is one thing we must remember: we must surrender control to the Lord. At the end of the day, the lives and times of our children are in His hands, just the same as ours. A sword pierced Mary's heart when her Son was taken away from her by God's plan, but still, she said, "I am my Lord's handmaiden, let it be done to me according to your word." As hard as it is, we must be willing to trust God and *know* that He is good. We must be able to say, "The Lord gives, and the Lord takes away, *blessed* be the Name of the Lord."

Prayer for Your Children:

Father in the Name of Jesus, I praise You for Your love and faithfulness. I thank You, oh God for giving Your angels charge over our children. According to Acts 16:31, *"If we believe in You, we will be saved, and our household will be saved."* Father, I trust in You and only You. Your Word declares in Proverbs 22:6, *"Train up a child in the way they should go, and when they are old they will not depart from it."* Thank You, Father, for the wisdom on how to lead, teach and pray for our children.

Father in the Name of Jesus, I declare that I am strong in the Lord and His mighty power. I put on all of

God's armor around our children, to protect their minds from any accusations, attacks, lies, schemes, temptations, peer pressure, tricks so that they will be able to stand firm against all the strategies of the Devil. For we are not fighting against flesh and blood, but against evil rulers and authorities of the unseen world, against mighty powers in this dark world, and against evil spirits in the heavenly places. *"Therefore, I put on every piece of God's armor around our children, so they will be able to resist the enemy in the time of evil"* (Ephesians 6:10–18).

Father, Your Word declares that, "You will pour out Your Spirit upon our offspring and Your blessing upon our descendants." You promise if we ask, seek, and knock, you will give us goods in return. I ask you Oh God, to put a hedge of protection around our children. Father, I declare in the Name of Jesus, that our children will know and have a relationship with You. I declare they are blessed when coming in and when going out. They are not cursed, but blessed! They are above and not beneath. They are the head and not the tail. Father fill them with compassion, power, kindness, hope, faith, gentleness, joy, strength, love, mercy, creativity, visions, patience, peace, humility, and security, help them oh God to walk in Your Light and Truth.

I declare they are free and saved. They are free from molestation, low self-esteem, suicidal thoughts, and every negative thought. I come against homosexuality, self-doubt; they will not doubt themselves, they will

not doubt the Holy Spirit, I come against it now in the
Name of Jesus. Father cleanse their minds of everything
that holds them bound.

Father, we come against, rebuke, bind and cast out
the power of the Devil and his fallen angels in the life
of our children. Father in the Name of Jesus, I break and
destroy any and all curses, spells, evil wishes, evil desires,
lies, obstacles, deceptions, spiritual influences, and every
dysfunction and disease from any source whatsoever, that
have been placed upon our children.

We pull down every stronghold that will hinder them
from serving You. For it is written, "*Let the little children
come to me and do not hinder them, for to such belongs the
kingdom of heaven* (Matthew 19:13–14)." Father, give
them the Spirit of wisdom, revelation, and a servant's
heart, so that they may know You better. I declare that
doors of opportunity shall become open in the lives of
our children. Father God, Your Word declares that You
have placed before us an open door that no one has the
power to shut. I command the doors of supernatural
favor to open unto our children in the Name of Jesus. I
declare everything they touch will prosper and succeed
according to Your perfect will.

I seal this prayer in the Name of Jesus
Amen!

Sixteen

PRAYER FOR FAMILY

"A family that prays together stays together."

"You shall love the Lord your God with all your heart, with all your soul, and with all your strength. And these words which I command you today shall be in your heart. You shall teach them diligently to your children, and shall talk of them when you sit in your house, when you walk by the way, when you lie down, and when you rise up. You shall bind them as a sign on your hand, and they shall be as frontlets between your eyes. You shall write them on the doorposts of your house and on your gates."

DEUTERONOMY 6:5–9

Prayer for Family:

Father in the Name of Jesus, I thank you for waking us up to see another day. Father guide us, protect us and watch over us as we make our rounds today. I declare that we are more than a conqueror through Jesus Christ (Romans 8:37), and everything we touch shall be blessed. I declare supernatural increase, supernatural miracle, favor, wealth, riches, power, and influence in our family in the Name of Jesus. We are favorable in the sight of God, and men. Father, as you clothed the children of Israel with favor, we too are clothed with the favor of God in the Name of Jesus! I declare that we are wearing a coat of many colors.

Father, we decree and declare that we can do all things through Jesus Christ who strengthens us. We are empowered to walk as children of light; bringing light into darkness. Help us to grow where we are planted that our areas of influence will increase. When we speak, we will speak with boldness, and people will pay attention to what we have to say. May Your glory shine on us so brightly, that even prominent people of our society will gravitate towards us providing an opportunity for us to share Your Word.

Father, teach us, Oh God, how to discern what is good and bad. Paul says that hard food belongs to those whose senses have been exercised to discern between good and evil. If there is ever a time for this level of discernment to be practiced, it is now. Equip us with the wisdom to identify Your will in every area of our lives, with absolute clarity. Teach us to live according to Your will. Father, show us Your ways, teach us Your paths and lead us in truth. Give us the strength and tenacity to walk according to Your precepts, and not stray from them to the left or the right. May we say like Joshua, as for me and my house, we will serve the Lord.

I declare that we are the children of the King! We are clothed with godly strength and dignity! We are loved! I declare that we are blessed and not cursed. We are the head and not the tail. We are rich and not poor. We are healed not sick. I declare that we are free! We receive freedom and peace today because our mind has been renewed.

No weapon of Satan and his agents formed against us shall prosper, in the Name of Jesus. Every tongue that rises against us in judgment will come under condemnation. We cloth ourselves with garments of righteousness, confidence, self-worth, dignity, humility, and meekness. I bind all ungodly spirit of rejection, distraction, isolation, death, violence, insecurity, peer pressure, and every other evil spirit working against our destiny. Our divine purpose is sealed. Activate the kingdom of God within us that we may walk in the power and authority You have given us to live in freedom, to bind up the brokenhearted, provide comfort to those who grieve, strength and encouragement to those who are oppressed and to set the captives free, in Jesus' Name.

I seal this prayer under the precious Blood of Jesus. Amen!

Seventeen

PRAYER FOR HUMILITY

"For whoever exalts himself will be humbled, and whoever humbles himself will be exalted."

MATTHEW 23:12

IN LUKE 18, JESUS contrasted the prayers of a Pharisee with that of a tax collector. One man sought God on the merit of his own good works and righteousness, but the other, the despised tax collector, sought God in repentance and humility. It was the prayer of the tax collector that was honored and upheld by Jesus. As you pray, seek the power of the Holy Spirit with humility and reverence, and God will answer your prayers. When you walk in humility before the Lord your God, the Holy Spirit will empower you to stand up against and resist your adversary so that the Devil flees from you. Satan operates in pride, but when you humble yourself under God's hand, Satan cannot work against you because he has nothing to hold on to.

Obey the promptings of the Holy Spirit, even if you do not understand. You do not need to understand the ins and outs of the situation you are praying for. God knows, and that's enough. If He has prompted you to do something, it is because He knows that you can do it. Trust and obey Him. Have faith in Him and see how He ministers to your life and the lives of those around you. *"Be on alert . . . pray in the spirit at all times"* (Ephesians 6:18).

Prayer for Humility:

Father in the Name of Jesus, I thank You for a humble heart. It is in humility that You exalt those who belong to You. I confess my sins and the sins of my ancestors. Wash us in the precious Blood of Your Son, Jesus Christ. Purify our hearts, Lord, and teach us how to walk humbly with You. You are God of the heavens and God on the earth. Your Word declares, *"Heaven is Your throne, and earth is Your footstool"* (Isaiah 66:2b).

According to 2 Chronicles 7:13–16, *"If I shut up heaven and there is no rain, or command the locusts to devour the land, or send pestilence among My people, if My people who are called by My name will humble themselves, and pray and seek My face, and turn from their wicked ways, then I will hear from heaven, and will forgive their sin and heal their land. Now My eyes will be open and My ears attentive to prayer made in this place. For now, I have chosen and sanctified this house, that My name may be there forever; and*

My eyes and My heart will be there perpetually." I present my body, my eyes, my tongue, my hands, and my feet as a living sacrifice, holy and acceptable to You, which is my spiritual worship. I will not allow or choose to let any member of my body, Your holy temple, be used in an ungodly fashion. I declare that I will not be conformed to this world, but be transformed by the renewal of my mind. I confess that I belong to You, oh God. Let me become more and more like You.

I declare that I am clothed with humility. For it is written, "*God resists the proud, but gives grace to the humble. Therefore, I humble myself under the mighty hand of God, that He may exalt me in due time.*" (1 Peter 5:5–6) We command every stronghold to be broken. We take authority and shut the door over the spirits of pride, self-praise, and self-exaltation in the Name of Jesus. Father, according to Your Word, "Pride goes before destruction, and a haughty spirit before a fall." Therefore, I resist and rebuke any demons of pride, self-willed, false holiness, and self-righteousness in the Name of Jesus.

According to Matthew 23:12, "*Whoever exalts himself will be humbled, and whoever humbles himself will be exalted.*" Father, I humble myself before You, fill me with the power of the Holy Ghost that I may be a witness to the gospel of Jesus Christ. "*Create in me a clean heart, O God; and renew a right spirit within me. Restore to me the joy of Your salvation and grant me a willing spirit, to sustain me*" (Psalm 51:10&12).

It is in humility that we truly learn to forgive and to seek mercy for a decadent society that deserves judgment. May You be merciful, and not treat us as our sins deserve, or repay us according to our iniquities. May we remain humble in the face of such overwhelming and undeserved grace.

In Jesus' Name.

Amen!

EIGHTEEN

PRAYER FOR SPIRITUAL VICTORY

"He was wounded for our transgressions, He was bruised for our iniquities; the chastisement for our peace was upon Him, and by His stripes we are healed."

ACCORDING TO ISAIAH 53:5

STAY IN YOUR ARMOR and use the power of the Word. Set your boundaries and claim your territory. Guard it and stand as a watchman over it. Protect your borders and prevail in your fight through the power of God. Serve Him with all your heart and your mind and fight for Him with all your strength. Through it all, through every victory and every defeat, praise the Lord and give Him the glory for He alone reigns in the storm, in the quiet, in the clamor, and the still of the night. He is God, and it is to Him and Him alone that we live or die.

God is all you have. Throw yourself at His feet, lean on His chest, avail yourself of His strength repeatedly as many times as necessary until you rout the enemy. Whatever the cost, however long it takes. Victory is yours because He has won the victory for you. The enemy is seeking to steal that victory from you, but it is up to you to enforce it and live the life of abundance. Do not allow the enemy to destroy you or trample on your territory. Do not depend on yourself or you will drown in the waves like Peter almost did. Through the power of the Spirit and the strength of God, you will rise to victory, every time.

Prayer for Spiritual Victory

"Lift up your heads, O you gates! And be lifted up, you everlasting doors! And the King of glory shall come in. Who is this King of glory? The Lord strong and mighty, the Lord mighty in battle. Lift up your heads, O you gates! Lift up, you everlasting doors! And the King of glory shall come in." (Psalm 24:7–9)

"Father, there is none that is powerful, as You. I praise and worship You. Your name is Wonderful, Counselor, Mighty God, Everlasting Father, and the Prince of Peace. There is truly no other god like my Jehovah.

Father, we thank You for the victory. I declare, we are more than conquerors through Christ that loves us, and we give thanks to God, who gives us the victory through our Lord Jesus Christ." (Romans 8:37; 1 Cor. 15:57)

I declare that we are covered with the full armor of God, which He has provided for all believers, knowing that we wrestle not against flesh and blood but against the rulers, against the authorities, against the powers of this dark world and against the spiritual forces of evil in the heavenly realms. The battle is not ours, but it is the Lord's—for it is not by my might, nor by my strength, but by the Spirit of God that I have the victory. Jesus, You have already won the victory and put to shame all our enemies.

Father in the Name of Jesus, I claim victory over sexual abuse, child abuse, shame, robberies, unfaithfulness, perversion, pride, envy, jealousy, unforgiveness, bitterness, wickedness, gossip, and a host of other things. I break free from the bondage of insecurity. Father, You are in control of my every step. I declare that I don't have to worry about tomorrow because Your Word says, *"The steps of a good man are ordered by the LORD: and he delighted in his way"* (Psalm 37:23).

I have all authority over Satan and all demons. We walk around the wall of Jericho and claim our victory, in the Name of Jesus. And we know that all things work together for good to them that love God, to them who are the called according to His purpose. For whom He did foreknow, He also did predestinate to be conformed to the image of His Son, that He might be the firstborn among many brethren. Moreover, whom He did predestinate, them He also called: and whom He called, them He also justified: and whom He justified, them He also glorified. What shall we then say to these things? If God be for us, who can be against us? (Romans 8:28–31)

I claim a hedge of protection around myself, my spouse, my children and my loved ones; I declare that we are not defeated, and victory belongs to us. The Bible tells us that, we are hard-pressed on every side, yet not crushed; we are perplexed, but not in despair (2 Corinthians 4:8).

I seal this prayer in the power of the Holy Spirit Amen!

NINETEEN

PRAYING AGAINST UNCLEAN SPIRIT (DEMONS)

And He said to them, "Go into all the world and preach the gospel to every creature. He who believes and is baptized will be saved; but he who does not believe will be condemned. And these signs will follow those who believe: In My name they will cast out demons; they will speak with new tongues."

MARK 16:15–17

YOU MUST UNDERSTAND THIS one thing before you can advance in prayer: you have no power and no authority on your own. You can command demons, Satan, and angels day and night until your voice is gone but if you are doing it because of the power of your voice, the power of your strength, the power of your spirit, you will only be laughed at and attacked even the more by the enemy. If you do not have a relationship with Christ then what happens is, you do not understand His power, you have never really been exposed to the true power of God, you are using a facsimile of what the power is, and nothing is more powerful than the original. Before you can cast out demons, you must do as the book of Romans demands us to do, *"renew your mind."* Because *"as a man thinketh so is he"* whatever you are you speak it with authority because you are made in God's image, you are created for authority. Demons know this. So, they are on a mission to pervert your authority in your mind. While casting out a demon, it will only respond to authority. Remember, demons know Jesus' authority without him saying a word. Demons only respond to whoever understands their authority. And that only comes from a relationship with Christ.

Look at what happened to the seven sons of Sceva in Acts 19. These men saw the power of God displayed in the works of Paul and they too desired to free people from the chains of demons. So, they told the demons to come out of those they afflicted "by the Jesus, whom Paul proclaims." But one spirit turned right around and said, "I know Jesus and I know Paul but who are you?" "And the man in whom was the evil spirit leaped on them, mastered all of them and overpowered them so that they fled out of that house naked and wounded."

The Sons of Sceva made one critical error—they called on the power of the Name of Jesus, but they themselves were not called by the Name of Jesus. Do you see the difference? Even demons can say the Name of Jesus, so can any number of unbelievers but until and unless you are called by Jesus' Name, you have no power or authority to use His Name. You have no power over the enemy except the authority Jesus has given you, and you have no access to Jesus until you are truly saved and have confessed your sins to Him.

Praying Against Unclean Spirits (Demons):

Father in the Name of Jesus, I repent of all my sins. I ask You, oh God, to forgive me of any distrust, dishonesty, jealousy, judging, pride, theft, greed, spiritual adultery or fornication, in the Name of Jesus Christ. According to Matthew 6:14, *"If you forgive other people when they sin against you, your heavenly Father will also forgive you."* Father, help me to forgive others as You forgive.

Father, you have given us the power and authority over all unclean spirits. I call forth legions upon legions of angels from heaven in the Name of Jesus to station around me as I pray this prayer. I release the Archangels, "Michael" to stand on my right, "Gabriel" to stand on my left, "Uriel!" to stand before me, and "Raphael" to stand behind me, and pull out their swords and cut off the head of the enemy. Father in the Name of Jesus, send fire from the third heaven to consume every demonic power that has been sent to destroy, to overpower and to frustrate us today. By the holy and precious Name of the Almighty God, everything that the enemy has illegally stolen from us, I command it to be released in the Name of Jesus.

According to Matthew 18:18, whatever I bind on earth will be bound in heaven, and whatever I loose on earth will be loosed in heaven. I take authority and bind every principality in high places, spiritual wickedness, rulers of darkness, and all the strong demons in the Name of Jesus. Let the Fire of the Holy Ghost destroy the python spirit, the cobra spirit, and its demons of witchcraft, divination, mind-control, heaviness, confusion, frustration, black magic, white magic, depression, and oppression.

Father, in the name of Jesus, I come against the spirit of Behemoth (the male) sea monster and Leviathan, (the female) [Esdras 6:48–52.] serpent, the large monster of the deep, the water spirits that work with the Jezebel spirit. According to Psalm 74:13–14, *"You divided the sea by Your strength; You broke the heads of the sea serpents in the waters. You broke the heads of Leviathan in pieces, and gave him as food to the people inhabiting the wilderness."* Therefore, I call on the power of the Holy Ghost to destroy Behemoth (the male) sea monster, Leviathan (the female) sea monster and the prince of all the demons, that cause, arrogance, lying tongue, murder, wickedness, depression, competition, helplessness, false witness, and death. Father, we decree and declare that the spirits that You hate are destroyed out of our lives, our children's lives, and our loved ones' in the Name of Jesus (Proverbs 6:16–19).

Father Your Word declare, *"When an unclean spirit*

goes out of a man, he goes through dry places, seeking rest and finds none. Then he says, 'I will return to my house from which I came. And when he comes, he finds it empty, swept, and put in order. Then he goes and takes with him seven other spirits more wicked than himself, and they enter and dwell there; and the last state of that man is worse than the first" (Matthew 12:43–45). I decree in the Name of Jesus these spirits shall not control us. I close every open door of bitterness, jealousy, slander, envy, that is in my heart towards anyone. The Word declares that whom the Son sets free is free indeed.

I decree and declare in the Name of Jesus that we will not be harmed by the spirit of Beelzeboul, the ruler of demons, Judas, Pharaoh, Jezebel, Ahab, Absalom, Herod, Hamman, and Cain in the Name of Jesus. *"Let God arise, and His enemies be scattered"* (Psalm 68:1). I come against every spirit that is under the control of the Leviathan spirit. I decree that the mind-controlling spirits, the seductive spirit, and the spirit of anxiety are destroyed in the Name of Jesus. I reiterate, whom the Son sets free is free indeed. I declare we are free!

I seal this prayer in His Blood, the Word, and the Spirit in Jesus' Mighty name.

Amen!

TWENTY

PRAYER FOR PEACE OF MIND

"The name of the LORD is a strong fortress; the godly run to him and are safe."

PROVERBS 18:10

EVERY DAY WE ARE inundated with stress, worry, and anxiety. It seems like everywhere we turn there is another thing to worry about. We remind ourselves that God has said that we can trust Him, and we do not have to worry, but we worry anyway. It's like a rite of passage from the worry-free days of childhood into adolescence and then later into adulthood.

There is another rite of passage that we must learn if we are to walk in the freedom and victory Christ promises. Worry and trust cannot abide together. If you are worried or anxious about something, you are not trusting God, no matter how much you say you trust Him.

The only person that can teach us to trust is the Holy Spirit. It is the work of God's grace in our hearts to teach us to trust in Him when we submit to Him. Peace of mind, freedom from worry and anxiety are the promises of God to those who run to Him for shelter and protection in these troubled times.

Prayer for Peace of Mind

Father God, I come to You in the mighty Name of Jesus. I delight myself in You, Lord. According to Psalm 28:7, *"The Lord is my strength and my shield; my heart trusts in him, and he helps me. My heart leaps for joy, and with my song I praise him."* You are my bright morning star. You are the Prince of Peace. Your Word declares that You will keep us in "perfect peace" if we keep our hearts fixed on You (Isaiah 26:3). Father my heart is full of agony, therefore, I come before Your throne to rejoice. In the midst of my sorrow, I declare and decree that I am happy because God is my refuge. I receive joy because the joy of the Lord is my strength. I receive peace, because Your word declares, in Philippians 4:6–7, I should *"be anxious for nothing, but in everything by prayer and supplication, with thanksgiving, let your requests be made known to God; and the peace of God which surpasses all understanding, will guard your hearts and minds through Christ Jesus."*

Father God, I praise and worship You in the day of trouble. Your word is a lamp to my feet, and a light to my path (Psalm 119:105). I declare that I will not fear the terror of night, nor the arrow that flies by day. You're the strength of my life; of whom shall I be afraid? *"Though an "army" should encamp against me, my heart shall not fear: though war should rise against me, in this will I be confident (Psalm 27:3-6).* I decree and declare that a thousand will fall at my side, and ten thousand at my right hand, but calamity will not come near to where I live.

I declare that Satan and his principalities and powers are defeated in the Name of Jesus Christ. I speak to the demonic spirits who try to take away my peace; I command you in the Name of Jesus to "Go!" Every oppressive spirit that is attacking my mind, I command you to "Go" in the Name of Jesus Christ. I command the spirit of fear, resentment, depression, and bitterness to go in the Name of Jesus. If God is for us, who can be against us? We are more than conquerors through Christ who loved us. For I am convinced that neither death nor life, neither angels nor demons, neither the present nor the future, nor any powers, neither height nor depth, nor anything else in all creation, will be able to separate us from the love of God that is in Christ Jesus (Romans 8:37-39).

I decree and declare that I will not be moved by any adverse problems, issues or circumstances. I declare that I will forever be happy, joyful, and full of God's love. I declare I have a peaceful mind, and I will maintain a godly perspective in every situation I face. Let God arise and let the enemy be scattered. "Peace, be still." In Jesus Name.

Amen!

Twenty-One

I BELIEVE PRAYER

THE BIBLE TELLS US in Mark 11:24, *"Therefore I tell you, whatever you ask for in prayer, believe that you have received it, and it will be yours."*

We are not just to pray, but rather to pray believing. If we are specifically told to believe when we pray, then it must be possible to pray and not believe. Not all prayer brings results. Only believing prayer moves the hands of God. Believing takes the attention from prayer itself and puts the attention entirely on God Himself. It is all about Christ and His faithfulness. The Bible does not teach us to rely on prayer alone. Nevertheless, it teaches us to rely on Him. Only when we fully rely on Christ can we fully pray believing. We are to believe in Him first, and then express that belief in prayer. Your faith must be in your heart before any prayer can come out of your mouth. When we pray, our prayers must line up with His Word. The only prayer that God will hear and answer is a prayer that is based on what He has said in His Word. If you pray according to the Word of God, then you are praying the will of God.

But what does it say? "The word is near you, in your mouth and in your heart"—that is, the word [the message, the basis] of faith which we preach—because if you acknowledge and confess with your mouth that Jesus is Lord [recognizing His power, authority, and majesty as God], and believe in your heart that God raised Him from the dead, you will be saved. For with the heart a person believes [in Christ as Savior] resulting in his justification [that is, being made righteous—being freed of the guilt of sin and made acceptable to God]; and with the mouth he acknowledges and confesses [his faith openly], resulting in and confirming [his] salvation. Romans 10:8–10 (AMP)

If you want Jesus (the Master) to change your life, if you want Him to change you completely, if you want to surrender ALL to Him, then you must believe that your prayer has POWER, you must believe that you have AUTHORITY, you must believe that all things work together for good for them that love Him.

Repeat this prayer after me and watch your life change forever.

I Believe Prayer:

Father, I give you my heart, my life, my health, my family, my marriage, my relationships, my ministry, my successes, and my failures. I surrender ALL to You, Oh God. May

You determine the course of my life from now onwards; the situations that I will face, and the people who will come into my life. I want to be Spirit-led. Open my ears to hear what You are saying in this season of my life, and open my eyes that I will behold Your glory. Cleanse me from the crown of my head to the sole of my feet with the Blood of Your Son. Purify my mind and imagination that I will receive messages with clarity. I decree and declare that I am a vessel of honor, worthy to be used by You. I confess that I belong to Jesus Christ, the Son of the Most High God forever, and I am His forever, and I am born again!

Jesus, I believe in You and receive You as my Lord, my Savior, my King, my Redeemer, and my Ruler. I believe you are Jesus Christ, the Son of the Living God. I believe in fervent prayer based on Scriptures. I believe in fasting. I believe the Bible is true and the Word of God. I believe that I should study to show myself approved, that I will never be ashamed.

I believe I am the lender and not the borrower. I am blessed coming in and blessed going out. I am the head and not the tail, I am above and not beneath. I believe I am blessed in the city and blessed in the field. [Deut. 28:2–13–14]

I believe You are my Jehovah-Jireh, (my provider), my Jehovah-Rapha, (my healer), my Jehovah-Nissi; my banner [Exodus 17:15–16].

I believe, with God all things are possible. Therefore,

I walk today expecting God's favor and success to be upon me! I believe there is nothing too hard for me to do because I believe in God. [Mark 9:23]

I believe He is above all principality and power, and virtue and dominion, and every name that is named not only in this world but also in that which is to come (Ephesians 1:20–21).

I believe the floodgates of heaven are opened for me, and I am receiving a blessing that I cannot contain. I believe that God has destroyed the devourer for my sake. [Mal 3:10]

I believe my God shall supply all of my needs according to His riches in glory by Christ Jesus. [Phil 4:19]

I believe I am prospering in my marriage, in my relationships, in my ministry, in my business, and in every area of my life. Whatever I touch is blessed. [Hebrews 11:1] I believe faith is confidence in what we hope for and assurance about what we do not see.

I believe Jesus has redeemed me from the curse of lack and poverty and want. I believe in the blessing of Abraham. I am blessed because of Him! [Gal 3:13] I believe, I am blessed, in the Name of Jesus!

I believe, He ascended into heaven and is seated at the right hand of the Father. [Mark 16:19].

I believe, every good and perfect gift is from above, coming down from the Father of the heavenly lights. [James 1:17]

I believe, the peace of God, which surpasses all understanding, will guard my hearts and minds through Christ Jesus. [Philippians 4:7]

I believe, whatever I ask in prayer, I will receive, because I have faith [Matthew 21:22].

In Jesus Name!

Amen!

CONCLUSION

Making Prayer a Daily Part of Your Life: Approaching the Father

Prayer is, at its heart, an intimate conversation with the Father. Intercession is a battle fought on your knees, in the throne room, for the citizens of the kingdom and for those held captive by the enemy. Neither of these calls for stilted, formal language. Approach your Father as a child would a parent. You would ask your father, "Daddy, can I get ice-cream?" rather than "Oh most gracious Daddy, do thou deem me worthy to receive thy kindness and favor? If I, thy humble child, have found favor in thine eyes, please bestow upon me the token of ice-cream." It is ridiculous, is it not?

Your heavenly Father loves you and loves to spend time with you. There is no need for flowery, over the top language or formal requests. Does your friend need help with a problem? Ask Him to help her. Plain and straightforward.

Your Father already knows what's going on. Realize that and come to Him with the request that is in your heart, talk to Him as you would talk to someone who was intimately familiar with your situation. If you were speaking to a stranger, you might give them background information and different details because they have no idea what you are talking about or whom you are referring to. On the other hand, if your sister asked if your mom would like something while she was in the hospital, you would not go into lengthy explanations of your mom's character or why she was there—your sister knew her and the situation. Instead, you would just tell her to bring your mom's hairbrush or favorite perfume or outfit. It is the same thing with God. Present your requests openly and genuinely. You do not need to be formal or stiff. Realize that God wants to hear your heart and your needs and He is ready to offer the answer.

You have just worked through a book that aims to guide and empower you in your prayer life. Whether you are battling the enemy or just speaking with Jesus, be honest about how you feel and what you want. Ask the Holy Spirit to show you how to pray for whatever situation you are praying over. Ask Him for wisdom and guidance to detect and thwart the plans of the enemy.

Making Prayer a Daily Part of Your Life: Fervency and Endurance

Pray with fervency and intensity, particularly when you

take up another's burden on your shoulders. Pray for their needs as if they were your own. When you pray, don't offer up empty platitudes or requests or senseless words. Be genuine, be earnest. Be sensitive as well, follow the Holy Spirit's lead, He is the one who came up with the battle plan, and He does not need you to deviate from it.

Endure in prayer. The battles are long and weary, but they must be fought. Our enemy is strong and resilient. He has been defeated, but he refuses to accept defeat and continues to taunt the believers and those who are his captives. Prevail in prayer so you can break their bonds on the saints and the prisoners. Endure until you enforce the victory in full.

Be alert. Stand your ground. Stay vigilant. Your adversary, the devil, prowls around like a roaring lion, seeking someone to devour (1 Peter 5:8).

The End and the Beginning of It All

The war is far from over and will not be over until you hear that trumpet sound, rending the heavens. When you hear that trumpet blast, roar in triumph with the angels because the war is won, and you, along with all the other saints—those who were slain in the line of duty and those who continued to fight will join the King once and for all. Satan will be thrown into the bottomless pit, and there will be no more tears, no more sorrows, no more pain. You will be in the city where God himself dwells. You will see Him, talk to Him, touch Him, and be with Him for all eternity.

This is what you are fighting for. Let this picture be forever before your eyes and even when you grow tired in the battle, look up to your Commander, your Beloved, and take strength. Press on, step forward for the Kingdom of God is suffering violence against it at the hands of the enemy, and you must battle for it forcefully. Therefore, you who have been called by His Name must be vigorous and steadfast. Prevail for the Lord your God and King!

NOTE:

We are living in an increasingly hostile world full of greed, deceit, and suffering. People are blinded by materialism, entrepreneurial behavior, and whatever is supported by these phenomena. It is therefore increasingly important to spread the Word of God and as it says in Matthew 28:19–20, *"Go therefore and make disciples of all the nations, baptizing them in the name of the Father and of the Son and of the Holy Spirit, teaching them to observe all things that I have commanded you; and lo, I am with you always, even to the end of the age."*

As God's mouthpiece, I say to the people of God, it is time to *"Stay Awake,"* it is time to wake up and put on the full Armor of Light. Seeking the Kingdom of righteousness and praying without ceasing are a significant partnership and aspect of daily living. Witches are praying, warlocks are praying, wizards are praying, sorcerers are praying, but whom are they praying to? What about God's people? Are you praying in the Name of Jesus? Is your Armor '*Shining Bright?*' Do you understand how vital it is to pray in the Name of Jesus? Jesus promises, "*And I will do whatever you ask in My name [as My representative], this I will do, so that the Father may be glorified and celebrated in the Son. If you ask Me anything in My name [as My representative], I will do it*" (John 14:13–14) AMP. Toward the end of His discussion, He said: "*Until this present time you have not asked a single thing in my name. Ask and you will receive, that your joy may be made full*" (John 14:6, 13, 14; 16:24). Praying in Jesus' Name honors Him. More importantly, praying in Jesus' Name glorifies the Father, the one and only God who gave His only begotten Son that whosoever believes in Him should not perish, but have everlasting life (John 3:16). It is beneficial to pray in Jesus' Name.

ABOUT THE AUTHOR

Lenie Tibert, is an author, marriage enthusiast, an inter-cessory prayer warrior, and spiritual leader, she praises the Holy Spirit for birthing her with the inspiration to write. She is a woman after God's own heart. For this reason, she is on the mission of fulfilling Jesus Christ's vision: re-defining and restoring the purposes for marriage and family as His first institution.

Her works include Book I: *My Marriage Matter*, (Oct. 2015), Book II: *The Armor of Light*, (July 2018). Apostle Lenie is the Founder and Chairman of Lenie Tibert Ministries and the co-visionary founder of Nazarene International Ministries located in, South Florida. Please feel free to send her an email at ltibert11@gmail.com as she enjoys hearing from her devoted readers.

Many blessings to you!

Follow her at tibertministries.com

These 21 Powerful Prayers
Were Written
to Light up Your Path to Greatness
to Edify you,
to Inspire you,
and to Motivate you.

"*The night [this present evil age] is almost gone and the day [of Christ's return] is almost here. So let us fling away the works of darkness and put on the [full] armor of light*" (Romans 13:12 AMP).